Taliesin Evans

All About the Midwinter Fair, San Francisco

Taliesin Evans

All About the Midwinter Fair, San Francisco

ISBN/EAN: 9783744569955

Printed in Europe, USA, Canada, Australia, Japan

Cover: Foto ©ninafisch / pixelio.de

More available books at **www.hansebooks.com**

All About The Midwinter Fair

San Francisco

and

Interesting Facts Concerning California?

By Taliesin Evans

Price 25 cts.

Published by
W. B. Bancroft & Co
San Francisco.

Copyright 1894 by W B Bancroft

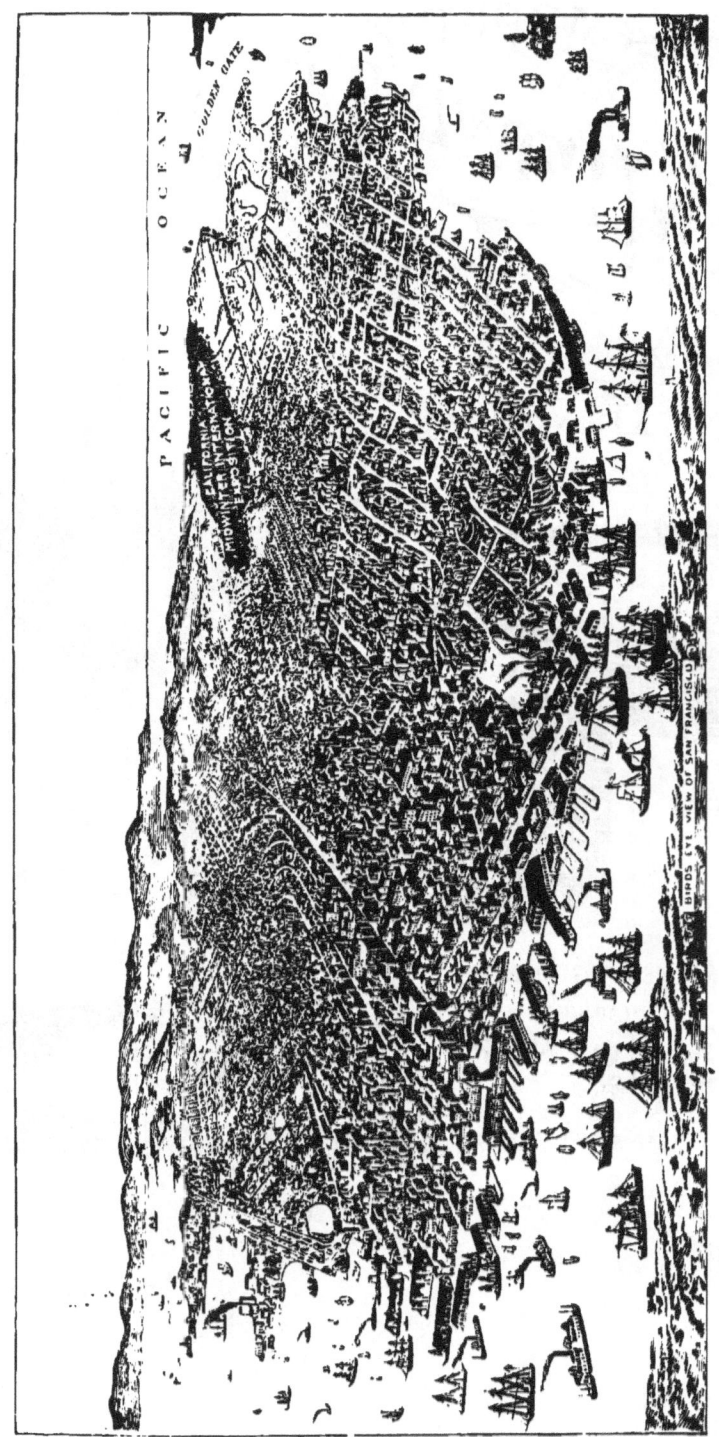

CALIFORNIA MIDWINTER INTERNATIONAL EXPOSITION

ALL ABOUT

THE

MIDWINTER FAIR

SAN FRANCISCO

AND INTERESTING FACTS CONCERNING

CALIFORNIA

BY

TALIESIN EVANS

PUBLISHED BY
W. B. BANCROFT & CO.

THE TRADE SUPPLIED BY
THE SAN FRANCISCO NEWS CO.

SAN FRANCISCO, CAL., U. S. A.

DRINK

BOHEMIAN CLUB COFFEE
MOCHA-JAVA BLENDED

AUTOCRAT OF THE BREAKFAST TABLE

FLAVOR, UNIFORM QUALITY, STRENGTH

ACCEPT NO SUBSTITUTE
INSIST ON THIS BRAND

Packed only in 1, 2½, and 5 lb. Cans—NEVER IN BULK

Sold by all the Leading Grocers at 40 Cents per Pound

AUTHOR'S PREFACE.

THE mission of *All About the Midwinter Fair* is to provide visitors to the California Midwinter International Exposition of 1894 with a convenient and reliable guide to all places of interest within the Fair grounds and in San Francisco and its environs, and to furnish them with such information concerning the resources and attractions of the Golden State as will be of service to them while sojourning here and of interest to them, possibly, after returning to their homes. The information contained in it has been carefully prepared and it has been arranged in a way handy for ready reference. Strict attention has been given to conciseness as well as to correctness of statement, so that the reader may not be wearied by prolixity nor worried through being misled by erroneous information. The maps and illustrations included will be found instructive as well as useful. A comprehensive index has also been provided, and the size and shape of the book have been made to fit the pocket without encumbering it.

The visitor to the Midwinter Exposition will, therefore, find in *All About the Midwinter Fair* a friendly medium for the removal of most of the troublesome annoyances and perplexities which are liable to be encountered in his ramblings without its assistance.

Residents of California will find within the covers of this handbook just such information concerning the State, San Francisco and the Midwinter Fair as they would desire to communicate to their friends abroad, by whom it will, without doubt, be regarded as a very acceptable gift.

ILLUSTRATIONS.

	PAGE
Art Institute	37
Alcatraz	48
Arts (Fine) Building	80
Agricultural Building	70
Administration Building	68
Bird's-Eye View Fair	67
Benicia Ferry Boat	26
Baldwin Hotel	82
Bird's-Eye View San Francisco	cover
Bay Ferry Boat	27
Basket of Trout	17
Bell, Mission	3
Buttress of El Capitan	11
City Front	72
California, Map of	1
Chinese Vegetable Vender	42
Chinese Restaurant	40
Chinatown, Scene in	40
Crocker Residence	36
Chronicle Building	29
Crocker Block	29
California Poppies	8
Camping Out	9
Castle Crags	11
Capitan, El	12
California Trout Stream	16
California Trout	17
Chinese Opium Smoker	42
Chinese Opium Den	43
Chinese Joss House	43
Cliff House	44
California Ostriches	78
California Hotel	28
Children's Playground	59
Conservatory, Interior	62
City Front	72
Dragon Fly (tail piece)	23
Deck of Solano	26
De Young, M. H.	69
Drake's Cross	64
Eschscholtzias	8
El Capitan	11
Eagle's Nest (tail piece)	66
Fine Arts Building	80
Flood Residence	37
Ferry Boat, Bay	27
Ferry Boat, Largest	26
First National Bank	31
Front, City	72
Golden Gate	cover, 25, 48
Guardians of the Gate	48
Hibernia Bank	90
Hotel Pleasanton	52
Hotel, Baldwin	82
Hotel, California	28
Hotel, Typical Family	52
Indians, Mission	2
Interior Conservatory	62

	PAGE
Kearny Street	63
Largest Ferry Boat	26
Liberal Arts Building	76
Lick Observatory	15
Looking Up Yosemite Valley	13
Manufacturers Building	76
Map of California	viii
Map North to Ukiah	96
Map South to Monterey	94
Mechanical Arts	74
Mark Hopkins' Institute	37
Market and Powell Streets	32
Model Bank	31
Mills Building	30
Market Street, at Post	29
Mission Bell	3
Mission Indians	2
Mission, San Antonio	2
Mount Shasta	11
Mount Shasta in Winter	14
Mission Dolores	47
Music Stand	56
New California	28
North Point	66
Observatory, Lick	15
Ostriches, California	78
Ocean Beach	61
Park Conservatory	cover, 60, 62
Park Scene	58
Poppies, California	8
Presidio Reservation	46
Pleasanton House	52
Playground, Children's	59
Rocks, Seal	cover, 44
Reservation, Presidio	46
Sutro Heights	61
Sharon Playground	59
Street Cars	54
Seal Rocks	cover, 44
Stanford Residence	36
San Antonio Mission	2
Shasta	11
Shasta in Winter	14
Stage, Yosemite	11
Stream, Trout	16
Speckled Trout	17
San Francisco Mission Church	47
Steamer Solano	26
Solano, Ferry Boat	26
Tail Pieces	23, 55, 66, 88, 92
Trout Stream	16
Trout	17
Yosemite Stage	11
Yosemite Valley	13
View Looking North	30
View of Kearny Street	63
Winter, Shasta in	14
Wild Flowers (tail piece)	55
Water Scene (tail piece)	88

CONTENTS.

	PAGE
Academy of Sciences	32
Adjacent Towns and Cities	48
Administration Building	6, 71
Admission of California	4
Adult Blind, Industrial Home	15
Agnews	14
Agricultural Building	72
Agricultural Products	4
Alameda County Building	77
Alameda, Population of	49
Alcatraz	49
Alcazar Theater	38
American Occupation	4
Amusements	38, 100
Amphibia, Santa Barbara	75
Angel Island	49
Anne Hathaway's Cottage	78
Art Association	39
Art Building	73
Asylums	14
Aviary	71
Baldwin Theater	38
Baseball Pitcher Statue	63
Bay Climate	51
Bay Ferries	26
Bay, San Francisco	47
Bay, San Pablo	48
Bay, Suisun	49
Big Facts	17
Big Farms	6
Biggest Ferryboat in the World	26
Big Orchards	6
Big Vineyards	6
Boarding Houses	52
Bohemian Club Coffee	ii
Boundaries Chinese Quarters	42
Boone's Arena	78
Branch Postoffices	35
Brothers, Two	48
Buffalo Paddock	58
Buildings, Fair	71
Buildings, Notable	30
Bureau, Hotel	52
Bush Street Theater	38
Byron Springs	94
Cable Railroads	54
Cabrillo's Voyage	1
Cairo, Streets of	77
California in Autumn	10
California Climate	7
California in Midwinter	8
California in Spring	8
California in Summer	10
California's Floral Emblem	8
California Theater	38
California, University of	15
Car (street) Fares	54
Carquinez Strait	26
Cazadero	95
Cemeteries	45
Charges Side Shows	79
Children's Park Playground	39, 58
Chinese Holidays	45
Chinese Quarters	40
Chinese Restaurant	41
Chinese Theaters	38, 42
Chinese Pagoda	75

	PAGE
Churches	39
City and County Buildings	33
City Hall	33
Cliff House	45, 51
Climate	7, 51
Clubs	38
Collections, Mineral, etc.	33
Commissioners, County	82
Commissioners, Foreign	84
Commissioners, State	82
Contents of the Park	57
Consuls, Foreign	87
Conservatory, Park	58
Cost Fair Buildings	81
Cost Park Improvements	58
Curios	33
Custom House	34
Deaf Mute and Blind Asylum	14
Deer Park	58
Del Monte	93
Descalso Bros.	109
Discovery of California	1
Divisions, Meteorological	7
Dolores, Mission	12, 51
Drake's Landing	64
Drake's Memorial	64
Drives in San Francisco	50
Early Fruits	5
Electric Tower	75
Entrances to Park	61
Esquimaux Village	78
Eschscholtzias	8
Establishments, Mission	2
Evening Bulletin	110
Exhibits, Foreign	73
Exposition Officers	69
Exposition Grounds	71
Fair Officers	69
Fair Buildings, Cost of	81
Farm, Ostrich	78
Farms, Big	6
Fathers, Franciscan	2
Ferries, Bay	26
Ferry Landings	28
Fine Arts Building	73
Finest Drive in the World	50
Firth Wheel	77
Flood Mansion	37
Floral Emblem (State)	8
Foreign Commissioners	84
Foreign Consuls	87
Foreign Exhibits	73
Forts in the Bay	23
Founding the Missions	2
Franciscan Fathers	2
French Library	39
Free Library	39
Free List at Fair	79
Friars, Franciscan	2
Fruit Districts	5
Fruit Growing	5
Game	15
Game Seasons	15
Garfield Monument	62
Gate, Golden	23
Gate Park, Golden	57
Gates of San Francisco	23

(v)

	PAGE
German Village	77
Geysers	94
Golden Gate	23
Gold Mining	4
Gold Product	4
Grand Drive	50
Ground Plan of Fair	98, 99
Hack Fares	53
Halleck Monument	62
Hammam Baths	102
Hawaiian Village	75
Hawaiian Cyclorama	75
Health Resorts	21
Heidelburg Castle	77
Heights, Sutro	51
History of Exposition	71
Horticultural Building	72
Hotel Bureau	52
Hotels	52
Houses, Boarding, etc.	52
How to Get to the Park	57
How to Get to the Springs	21
How to Get to the Resorts	21
Hydraulic Mining	4
Improvements, Park	58
Indians, Mission	2
Industrial Home Adult Blind	15
Inside Quadrangle	75
Interesting Collections	33
Itineraries	93
Jack Rabbit Hunting	15
Japanese Village	77
Junipero Serra	2
Kern & Elbach	103
Klinkner & Co., C. A.	103
Lassen Buttes	13
Leland Stanford, Jr., University	14
Libraries, San Francisco	39
Liberal Arts Building	72
Lick Observatory	14
Lighthouses, San Francisco	23
Lighthouse Station	49
Manufacturers' Building	71
Market Street, San Francisco	28
Mark Hopkins Institute of Art	37
Marshall's Discovery	4
Masonic Temple	31
Memorial Cross	1, 64
Mendocino, Named After	1
Metropolitan Artery	28
Michels, Wand & Co.	111
Midwinter Fair Buildings	77
Midwinter Fair Grounds	98, 99
Midwinter Fair, Origin of	71
Military Reservations	45
Mills Building	31
Mineral Springs	13, 21
Mining Camp	77
Mission Dolores	47
Mission Indians	2
Missions of California	2
Montague & Co., W. W.	back cover
Monterey Building	75
Montenegro	77
Monuments, Park	62
Mountain Scenery	10
Mount Diablo	11
Mount Shasta	10
Mount St. Helena	11
Mount Tamalpais	11
Mount Whitney	11
Moorish Maze	78
Municipal Buildings	33
Napa Soda Springs	94
Native Tribes	2
Natural Wonders	13
Needles	8
Neighboring Towns	49
Northern California	77

	PAGE
Notable Buildings	30
Oakland	48
Oakland Creek	27
Oakland's Population	49
Observatory, Lick	14
Odd Fellows' Hall	33
Officers' Exposition	69
Olive Culture	5
Orange Culture	6
Orchards, Big	6
Origin California	1
Origin Midwinter Fair	71
Ostrich Farm	78
Outside Quadrangle	75
Pagoda, Chinese	75
Park, Area of	57
Park Conservatory	58
Park Entrances	61
Park Improvements, Cost of	58
Park Monuments	62
Paraiso Springs	94
Paso Robles Springs	94
Peaks, Mission	49
Phelps & Dayton	107
Picturesque Russian River	97
Pioneer Building	32
Places Easy to Visit	93
Population Alameda	49
Population Berkeley	49
Population Oakland	49
Population San Francisco	24
Popular Resorts	21
Postoffices	34
Prater, Vienna	75
Presidio	45
Production of Gold	4
Products, Agricultural	4
Products, Horticultural	5
Providence Savings Life	102
Prune Districts	5
Public Libraries	39
Public Institutions (City)	33
Public Institutions (Federal)	34
Public Institutions (State)	14
Quadrangle, Inside	75
Quadrangle, Outside	75
Queretaro, Treaty of	4
Railroads, Street	54
Raisin Districts	6
Report, Daily	106
Resorts and Springs	21
Rocks, Seal	45
Roumania	77
Russian River Valley	95
Ryder, Mrs.	111
Salmon Fishing in the Sea	16
San Antonio Creek	27
San Francisco	23
San Francisco Amusements	38
San Francisco at Night	49
San Francisco Bay	47
San Francisco Climate	51
San Francisco Commerce	25
San Francisco Hack Fares	53
San Francisco Hotels	52
San Francisco Postoffices	34
San Francisco Surroundings	47
San Gorgonio Pass	8
San Pablo Bay	48
Santa Barbara Amphibia	75
Santa Clara Building	75
Scenery	10
Scenic Railway	77
School of Elocution	104
Scott Key Monument	63
Seal Rocks	45
Seasons	7
Servia	77
Shasta	10

	PAGE		PAGE
Side Shows	79	Transfers, Street-Car	54
Sioux Village	78	Travelers' Bureau	cover
Sleigh Ride	93	Trolling for Salmon	16
Social Clubs	38	Trout Fishing	16
Soldiers' Home	49	Trout Streams	16
Southern California Building	77	Two Brothers	48
Spanish Names	89	Union Photo-Engraving Co.	112
Space for Foreign Exhibits	73	United States Buildings	34
Spaulding & Co., J.	108	United States Appraisers' Stores	34
Special Celebrations	85	United States Courts	34
Stanford University	14	United States Mint	34
Stanford's Benefactions	6	United States Treasury	35
Starr King Monument	66	University of California	15
State Floral Emblem	9	Ukiah	97
State Institutions	14	Veteran's Home	49
State Prisons	14	Views from San Francisco	48
State University	14	Vineyard, Largest in the World	6
Strawberry Hill	61	Vineyards, Big	6
Street-Car Fares	53	Vienna Prater	75
Street Railroads	53	Waters, R. J.	109
Streets of Cairo	77	What the Park Contains	57
Suisun Bay	48	Wine Districts	6
Sunday at Fair	87	Wonder	105
Sutro Heights	51	Wonders of California	13
Taber Photographic Co.	101	Yerba Buena County	45
Tehachape	8	Yerba Buena Island	49
Torpedo Station	49	Yosemite Valley	11, 95
Tower, Electric	75	Yountville Veterans' Home	49

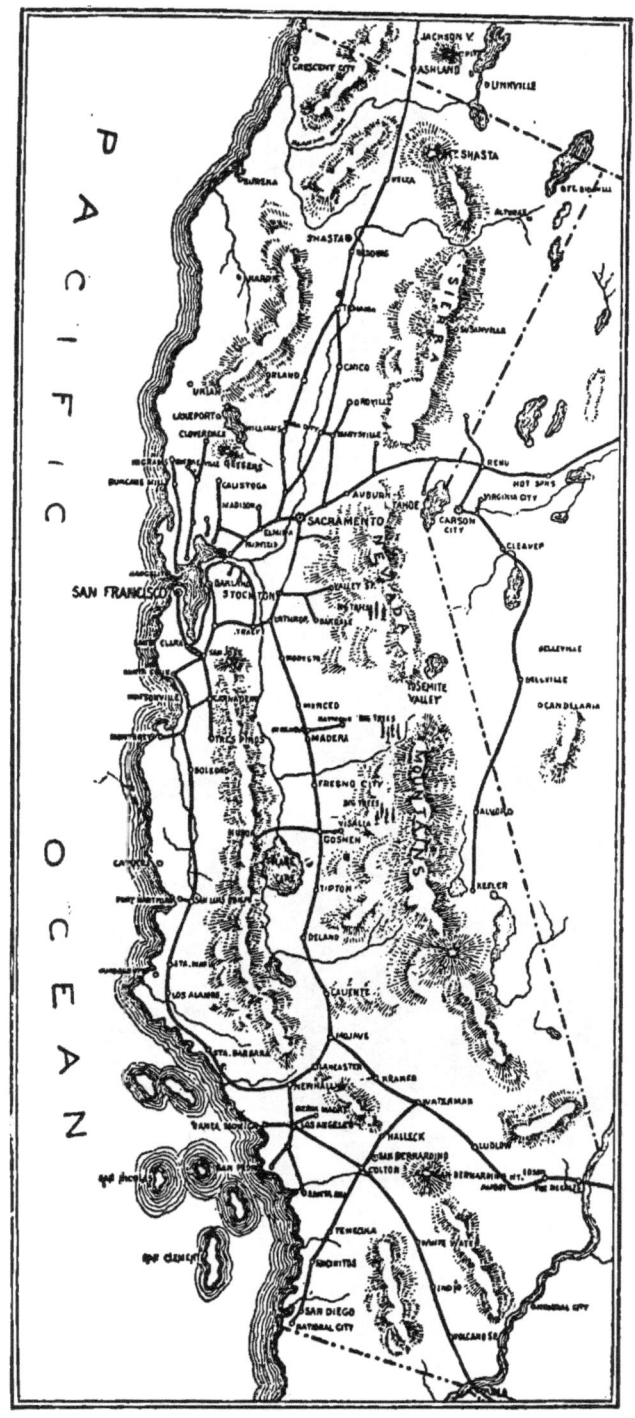

MAP OF CALIFORNIA

CALIFORNIA:

The Land of the Golden Sunset.

Origin of California—

The origin of California—the name of the Golden Sunset State—is obscure and uncertain. It was first applied in a Spanish romance, published in the sixteenth century, to an imaginary island in the Pacific Ocean. It was afterward attached by the Spaniards to the peninsula lying between the Gulf of California and the main body of the Pacific, now known as Lower California, which they found in their voyages of discovery during the time of Cortez. It was officially adopted in the State Constitution, framed, ratified and put into effect in 1849, nearly a year before Congress regularly admitted the State into the Union under the Act of September 9, 1850.

Discovery of California—

The Midwinter International Exposition of 1894 gives the visitor from abroad an opportunity to study California in a way that has never before been offered, under new and favorable conditions. At all times in its history this land of the Golden Sunset has been surrounded by a halo of romance. Cortez's explorations of the Gulf of California and the territory adjacent to it first excited the human imagination concerning the *terra incognito* lying farther north. The honor of its discovery rests, however, with Juan Rodriguez Cabrillo, a Portuguese navigator, who made a voyage along its shores in 1542 in the service of the Spanish Viceroy de Mendoza, and in whose honor Cape Mendocino, the most westerly headland on its coast, was named by the voyager. But Sir Francis Drake is believed to have been the first European to set foot on the shores of California. He is supposed to have landed at what has since been called Drake's Bay, near Point Reyes, in 1579. At the same time and place the first Christian service held on California soil was rendered by the Chaplain of Drake's flagship, and in commemoration of this event a massive granite memorial cross is being erected at Golden Gate Park, near the site of the Midwinter Exposition.

The Mission Era—

In 1769 the San Francisco friars, under the leadership of Father Junipero Serra, began the foundation of the California missions by the planting of the first establishment at San Diego. During the fifty-four years following they founded twenty other

SAN ANTONIO MISSION

institutions of the same order at various points between San Diego and Sonoma. Following is a complete list of the California missions and the date of their establishment: San Diego, 1769; San Carlos, 1770; San Gabriel and San Antonio. 1771; San

MISSION INDIANS

Luis Obispo, 1772; San Francisco (Mission Dolores) and San Juan Capistrano, 1776; Santa Clara, 1777; San Buenaventura, 1782; Santa Barbara, 1786; Purissima, 1787; Soledad, 1791; San Fernando, San Miguel, San Bautista, Santa Cruz and San Jose,

1797; San Luis Rey, 1798; Santa Inez, 1804; San Rafael, 1817; Sonoma, 1823. Many of these mission churches are now in ruins. Some of them have been repaired and partially restored in recent times, so as to fit them for re-occupation. They were originally designed as places of worship for the use of the native tribes which were then numerous, but living in a state of barbarism and spiritual darkness, and for whose conversion to Christianity the Franciscan friars devoted their lives. The civilizing

MISSION BELL.

influences thus brought to bear upon the Indians of California had, however, much the same effect upon them as such influences have had on the native races elsewhere on this continent, for their decline has been coincident with the decay of the churches erected for their benefit, and only a few of them are now to be found at any of the missions. At some of the old mission establishments they have disappeared altogether, and many of the mission churches which have been partially restored are now being used for worship by those who have succeeded them as occupants of the soil.

American Occupation-

In 1846 the American flag was raised at Monterey by Commodore Sloat, as a token of the occupation of the country by the United States. In 1848, at the conclusion of peace by the signing of the Treaty of Queretaro, Mexico formally ceded the territory now including the State of California to the United States. The same year, but at an earlier date, to-wit: on the 19th of January, John W. Marshall discovered gold at Sutter's Mill at Coloma, which brought the new territory into greater prominence than ever, resulting the following year in one of the most notable gold excitements which the world has ever witnessed. It is said that eighty thousand immigrants came to California in 1849, most of whom at once engaged in mining the rich gold placers, which extended over an area of about ten thousand square miles.

Gold Mining—

Gold mining has been prosecuted in California ever since Marshall's discovery was made, and although now occupying only a secondary place in the resources of the State, it yields annually from $15,000,000 to $20,000,000, and it has contributed to the world's wealth up to date the enormous sum of $1,300,000,000. The shallower placers have, of course, been exhausted long ago, and for over ten years the working of the deep-gravel deposits by the hydraulic process (a method of mining peculiar to the State) was nearly totally suspended by operation of law. Recent action by Congress providing for the impounding of the vast quantities of detritus which this process of mining releases and discharges into the beds of the navigable streams, has, however, made the resumption of hydraulic mining possible, and visitors to the Midwinter Exposition have abundant opportunity in the mining districts, in the northern part of the State, to witness this interesting industry, while exhibits of all the appliances employed in it are to be found in the Mining Department of the Fair. Just at present there is a great revival in progress also in gold quartz mining and many important developments have been the result. The visitor to the Midwinter Fair will find in the Mining section a display of the resources of the State in this respect and of other minerals found and profitably worked in the State, finer than has ever before been attempted in any country.

Agricultural Products—

The real development of California has occurred since the discovery of gold and through the agency of its fertile soil and genial climate. During the Mexican regime, and for the first two years of the American occupation, it was strictly a pastoral territory, its broad valleys and the sunny slopes of its mountain ranges being the pasturage of great herds of Spanish cattle, whose hides, tallow and horns constituted the chief articles of export. The great herds of Spanish cattle and the flocks of Merino sheep which succeeded them have long ago passed away, and for over twenty years past the State has been one of the largest wheat exporters in the world, the surplus products of its grain fields being shipped to feed the hungry millions of Great Britain and Continental Europe. But in recent years the horticultural and viticultural resources of the State have stepped to the front, eclipsing all others in value and variety. The horticultural products embrace, as is shown in the Agricultural and Horticultural Building at the Fair, all the varied range common to both the temperate and semi-tropical zones, soil and climate being equally favorable for their perfect development, and that in the greatest profusion. These fruits are shipped in the fresh and in the cured state in large quantities by rail and by sea to the Eastern and interior States and abroad, commanding special attention and good prices in the markets where sold, owing to their early development and superior quality.

Early Fruits—

A better conception of the adaptability of soil and climate to fruit culture may be obtained possibly from the fact that, with a brief interim of about six weeks in the beginning of the year, strawberries grown in the open air without the agency of any "forcing" medium, are purchasable in the markets the year round. In favored districts, north of San Francisco, ripe cherries have been shipped before the end of March; apricots at the end of April; peaches before the middle of May; apples and cherry plums following a few days later; figs at the end of May, and grapes before the close of June. And when the greater part of the United States is locked in ice and buried under a sheet of snow, this Western land of perennial sunshine and endless summer is placing in the markets of Eastern cities train-loads of golden fruit from its orange groves. Fruit growing has, naturally, become one of the chief industries of the State, and it is estimated that a capital of over $20,000,000 is actually invested in its orchards.

District Specialties—

Many districts in the State are devoted to the cultivation of special classes of fruit. For instance, prune growing is the chief orchard industry of the Santa Clara Valley. The principal cherry orchards of the State are in Alameda County, only an hour's ride from San Francisco. Apricots are made a specialty in the Vaca district. Fresno, Tulare and other counties in the San Joaquin Valley; Woodland and Winters in Yolo County; Auburn in Placer County and some sections of the southern part of the State constitute the raisin districts. The chief wine districts are in Napa, Sonoma, Alameda, Santa Clara, Sacramento, Tehama, Yolo, Fresno and Los Angeles Counties. The vintages of Livermore Valley in Alameda County have carried off some of the chief prizes in the Paris and Chicago Expositions, and the products of all the wine districts of California are in great favor in the Eastern States and in England, France and Germany. Olive culture finds a home in Santa Barbara, San Diego and Placer Counties, in each of which districts large tracts of land are devoted to the production of the fruit for oil making and pickling purposes.

Big Orchards, Vineyards and Farms—

The State is famous for its big orchards, vineyards and farms. The great Glenn wheat ranch embraces almost an entire county comprising between fifty and sixty thousand acres cultivated to cereals. The largest apple orchard in the world is at Novato, Sonoma County, and covers six hundred acres. The largest vineyard in the world is at Vina, Tehama County, comprising four thousand acres, and the next largest, the Natoma, near Folsom. The Vina ranch, of which the vineyard is a part, comprises fifty-five thousand acres of land which the late Senator Leland Stanford dedicated, in conjunction with the Gridley wheat ranch, embracing twenty-one thousand acres in Butte County, and the Palo Alto stock farm, consisting of seventy-three hundred acres in San Mateo County, and constituting the largest horse farm in the world, to the cause of higher education as represented in the Leland Stanford, Jr., University which is located thirty-three miles south of San Francisco. The largest fruit orchards in the State are those of General Bidwell of Chico, consisting of sixty-five thousand two hundred and fifty trees. Some districts are devoted to the raising of early vegetables for home consumption and shipment east and Santa Clara County supplies the entire United States with onion seed. The latter county has really the largest seed farms in the world, producing one-half the world's supply, shipping over three hundred tons annually, mostly to Europe.

Citrus Culture—

Contrary to popular impression abroad, citrus culture is not confined to the southern counties. Much of the region north of the Tehachepi Range is quite as well adapted for that purpose as the most favored localities in the south-land, the lime, lemon and orange flourishing there equally well. As a matter of fact and worth recording here, the earliest California oranges marketed are produced by the groves of the northern counties— at Oroville, Thermalito, Palermo, Newcastle, Winters and Vacaville. All of these places are north of San Francisco and some of them are situated in the foothills of the Sierra. In each of these places, the orange ripens three and four weeks earlier than it does in any part of the southern counties; and for size and quality the oranges of the northern groves have proven superior when brought into direct competition at the Citrus Fairs with those produced at Riverside and other southern orange districts.

California Climate—

It goes without saying, of course, that a State which yields prolifically such varied agricultural products must be possessed of an exceptionally mild climate. California comprises an area of 156,591 square miles of territory which extends through ten and one-half degrees of latitude, but the climate is practically isothermal throughout the greater part of it. The temperature the year round of the great central basin of the State, embracing the Sacramento and San Joaquin and tributary valleys, extending from the latitude of Santa Barbara to the base of Mount Shasta and comprising nearly one-third of the area of the State, is very similar to that prevailing in the southern counties. Over a vast area of this great basin, frost and snow are, in fact, unknown. The greater part of it possesses some meteorological advantages over the southern counties, in the fact that the annual rainfall is heavier and irrigation for the production of crops, whether they be fruits or grain, is unnecessary.

Meteorological Subdivision—

The State may be very fairly divided into three meteorological subdivisions: the coast district, comprising the territory lying between the summit of the coast ranges and sea which is somewhat humid and cool owing to the prevalence of fogs and proximity to the ocean; the central district, which may be embraced between two parallel lines following the summit of the inner Coast Range on the west and a corresponding elevation along the flank of the Sierra foothills on the east, from the foot of Shasta to the Lower California boundary line; and the mountain region comprised within the higher altitudes of the Sierra Nevada and other ranges lying within the snow and frost lines. But the area of the latter district is comparatively limited, and in the greater part of the State there are in reality only two seasons of the year —the wet and the dry. The former sets in usually in November and closes beginning of May. During the rest of the year rain very rarely falls in any part of the State.

California in Midwinter

There can be nothing more charming to the eye of the sight-seeing tourist than a California midwinter landscape, unless it be the same landscape in the spring. The hills and valleys are clothed with verdure brought forth by the early winter rains and furnishing abundant nutritious feed to the herds of fattening kine browsing upon them. The air is fragrant and fresh and vibrates with the twittering of the feathered tribe, while the purified atmosphere seems to give a clearer and longer perspective to the vision. If the tourist enters the State by either of the northern routes, the sudden change from the frost-bound realms of the storm and snow king into verdure-clad valleys and mountain ranges, is like an unexpected transition into Paradise; if the entrance be made through either of the southern portals—by way of the Needles and Tehachepi Pass, or by way of Fort Yuma and San Gorgonio Pass, the effect of the change from the monotonous

CALIFORNIA POPPIES

desolation of the desert to a land of luxuriance is the same. Reports of the richness of California's soil, the geniality of its climate and the grandeur and picturesqueness of its scenery may have been listened to heretofore with a strong suspicion lurking in the mind that the narrative was highly flavored with romance; but the testimony of the vision dispels the notion of fairy tales and they promptly assume the shape and status of glorious realities to the enchanted senses.

California in Spring—

But notwithstanding all the varied beauty of an average midwinter, the greater glory of California is manifested with the coming of Spring. It is then that the wild flowers, many-hued and fragrant, begin to unfold, bedecking every valley, mountain slope and wooded height with a gorgeous garment of many colors. Conspicuous among this varied floral group is the California poppy or eschscholtzia which, by common consent, has been adopted as the floral emblem of the State. This brilliant flower decorates meadow and mountain with great masses of gold and orange. The dainty green foliage of the manzanita and the ruddy tints of its flaming and distorted branches are smothered under a crown of delicate pink and white blossoms. The orchards burst forth in full bloom. The carefully pruned vineyards are

CAMPING OUT

again in leaf. The dark pine forests take on a new and brighter color; the tiger lily springs from its cover, and the tender blades of the growing grain leap from the brown earth as soon as it is deserted by the plow-boy and the harrower, quickly hiding it under an emerald mantle of wondrous richness. This is the aspect of nature as it is viewed by the tourist in California fresh from the reading of accounts of havoc and death waged by blizzards in the great Northwest, of the damaging effects of frost and flood and gale along the Atlantic seaboard and of the devastating work of cyclones and tornadoes throughout the central and southern group of States.

California in Summer—

Summer comes to California full grown at the close of the rainy season. It is the season of ripening. The verdure disappears from the face of the land with the same magical acceleration which brought it into being. The corrollas of the floral host wither and drop, and pod and petal and stalk shrivel under the heat of the sun. The grain fields whiten, ready for the harvester. The green pastures are turned to russet, and the beaded head of the wild oat grows gray. The fruits of orchard and vineyard mature and mellow; and every hand that has the strength to gather the harvest can find employment, and every available beast of burden and vehicle is required to transport it to market. This is the season when the toiling dwellers in cities and towns seek repose and recreation by camping out in secluded nooks and corners in the Coast Ranges and in the higher altitudes of the Sierra.

California in Autumn—

Then comes Autumn "crowned with the sickle and the wheaten sheaf," the most benignant season of the year. Calm, placid, tender and genial, it follows in the wake of Summer and lingers long in what would elsewhere be the lap of Winter. The cool ocean trade winds have died out, and the fierceness has passed out of the sun's rays. The hum of the vine press is heard through the land and the rich vintage is flowing into the vats. The later fruits are ripe for the gatherer, and the groves of the Hesperides are preparing to yield their golden apples. Autumn frequently prolongs its stay in California to "ring out the old year and to ring in the new."

Mountain Scenery—

California excels in mountain scenery, and it contains some of the most interesting high peaks on the continent. The fame of Mt. Shasta, the silent, snow-capped sentinel of the north, which elevates its cone-like head into the air 14,442 feet above the sea-level, is world-wide, and its neighbor — Castle Crags — although much inferior in height, has of late years attracted much of the attention of tourists, owing to its exceptional beauty and its picturesque surroundings. "Old Baldy," as Mt. San Bernardino is familiarly called, serves a similar purpose in the south to that of Shasta in the north, as it guards the southern gate to the State, rising in imposing grandeur above all its fellows in the Sierra Madre. About midway between these two peaks is Mt. Whitney, the monarch of the Sierra Nevada, 14,887 feet above the level of the sea, and constituting the highest elevation in the State. It stands in Inyo County, and is becoming famous as the source whence some of the finest marble obtained in California is quarried. Interesting peaks near San Francisco, well worthy the attention of tourists, are Mt. Diablo, standing in the heart of the inner Coast Range, twenty miles east of San

SHASTA AND CASTLE CRAGS

Francisco, plainly visible on a clear day, and from whose summit one of the finest views obtainable on the continent is brought within the range of vision, and Mt. St. Helena in Napa County, less than fifty miles due north of San Francisco. A fine view of land and sea is also obtainable on a clear day from the summit of Mt. Tamalpais, which is only a few miles' walk from the neigh-

A YOSEMITE STAGE

boring town of Sausalito, and it is easy of access at all seasons. But the Mountain Mecca of all tourists in California is the Yosemite Valley, situated in the heart of the Sierra Nevada, and reached from San Francisco by rail and stage in less than two days, and at a cost of less than $100 for the round trip. The ride by stage—the old-fashioned means of transportation still in vogue in many parts of the State, especially to many of the more popular resorts—is exceedingly interesting, the road passing, no matter which of the two routes into the valley is selected, through a wild and romantic region and giving the astonished tourist an opportunity of seeing those forest wonders, the giant Sequoias, and occasional glimpses here and there of the fascinating industry of gold mining in its varied forms. The Yosemite contains some of the most wonderful natural phenomena on the face of the

THE BUTTRESS OF EL CAPITAN

globe. The stupendous granite cliffs, walling in the great gorge and rising vertically from one-half to three-quarters of a mile high from the floor of the valley, are supported by buttressed domes and adorned with waterfalls of incomparable beauty, some of which have a clear, unbroken descent of nearly a thousand feet over the face of the cliff. A view up the great valley from Inspiration Point is one of the grandest ever enjoyed by the human eye.

CALIFORNIA—LAND OF THE GOLDEN SUNSET 13

The region of Lassen Buttes in the northeastern corner of the State is full of natural wonders, but it is seldom visited by tourists for the reason that it is remote from railroad communication and difficult to reach by other means of transportation. In the summer season the summit of Shasta tempts the courage and endurance of the tourist.

Natural Wonders—

The State is full of natural wonders of interest to the Eastern tourist. Mineral springs without number, hot and cold, some

LOOKING UP YOSEMITE VALLEY

suggestive of the realms above and others of the regions below; petrified forests, geysers and mammoth redwoods are within easy distance and accessible at trifling cost. Many of the mineral springs contain medicinal properties of great value, and a large number of them have in consequence developed into popular resorts.

Interesting State Institutions—

Tourists interested in the inspection of educational, penal, humane and scientific institutions can indulge their taste at trifling expense and with little loss of time during their visit to San Francisco. The University of California is located at Berkeley, three-quarters of an hour's ride by ferryboat and rail; the Leland Stanford Jr. University, constituting one of the most unique and handsome groups of collegiate buildings in the United States, is less than an hour's ride by rail. Lick Observatory, the gift of the late James Lick to astronomical science, can be reached by rail and stage in a few hours, as it is located twenty-six miles east of San Jose, whence it may be seen, on the summit of Mount Hamilton. This observatory contains, of course, the largest

MOUNT SHASTA IN WINTER

achromatic telescope in existence, the big lens having a diameter of thirty-six inches in the clear. Many discoveries of interest to astronomers, among them a fifth moon in the system of Jupiter, have been made at this observatory. At Agnews, also adjacent to San Jose, is an asylum for the insane; another is situated at Napa, and a third at Ukiah, Mendocino County. The student of penology may look into the California system at San Quentin, an hour's ride by ferryboat and rail from San Francisco, or at Folsom, Sacramento County, where he will also see one of the finest dams constructed in the United States for the development of power. The education of the deaf and dumb and blind is exemplified at the institution devoted to that purpose at Berkeley, adjacent to the University of California, and an Industrial Home for the Adult Blind is maintained by the State at Oakland.

LICK OBSERVATORY

Game—

The sportsman may indulge his love of the chase to his heart's content in almost any line of game he may desire. Of course the larger game, such as the grizzly and cinnamon bear, are found only in the fastnesses of the higher Sierras. Deer is plentiful in all of the mountain districts. Hares, or jackrabbits, are so numerous in the San Joaquin Valley that they have become intolerable pests and are slaughtered by tens of thousands yearly by driving them in droves into pens erected for the purpose. Cottontail rabbits and quail are plentiful in almost all the hills. During the winter months the marshes and rivers furnish good duck hunting and the plains of the upper Sacramento and its tributaries furnish fine sport in the way of wild geese. Under the State law the game season is open as follows: For deer, from September 1st to October 15th; quail, from September 1st to March 1st; doves, from August 1st to March 1st; wild duck, from September 1st to March 1st. In some of the counties the deer season begins in the month of July.

Fishing—

The State is famous among the followers of Isaac Walton for its fine fishing grounds. Trolling for salmon is a favorite pastime at certain seasons of the year in Monterey Bay, the only place in the open ocean in the world where this gamey fish is taken in salt water by means of a line. Almost every stream in the State is

A CALIFORNIA TROUT STREAM

stocked more or less abundantly with trout, affording fine sport for the angler, while many of the lakes teem with whitefish and speckled beauties. There are a great many good trout streams adjacent to San Francisco, but the best fishing and the largest fish are obtainable in the waters of the upper Sacramento and its tributaries. This State is the home of several species of trout not found elsewhere, and many of its streams and bays in late years have been stocked with the best game and food fishes of

Eastern waters. Visitors to the Midwinter Fair may test their skill as anglers in California streams and lakes, as the season begins April 1st and closes November 1st.

Big Facts in Short Dress—

California is larger than all the New England States, New York, New Jersey, Delaware and Maryland combined.

Railroads penetrate all the counties in the State except Modoc, Plumas, Lake, Tuolumne, Mariposa, Alpine, Trinity, Humboldt and Del Norte, and most of them will have railroad connection in a few years no doubt.

SPECKLED BEAUTIES

Monterey Bay contains a greater variety of fish than any other locality known, over 150 species being reported.

A squash weighing 283 pounds and measuring four feet in diameter is the largest recorded in the State.

There are over 3,000 artesian wells in the State.

Fourteen thousand gallons of olive oil and twelve tons of pickled olives is the record made in one season by a San Diego olive orchard.

Thirty cities and villages, in which one-half of the population of the State dwell, can be counted from the summit of Mt. Diablo.

The largest peach orchard in the State is near Yuba City, and it contains 575 acres.

Knight's Ferry, Stanislaus County, boasts of the finest and oldest fig orchard in the State, the trees in which are upwards of thirty years old.

The Alvarado, Alameda County, beet-sugar factory was the first refinery of the kind in the United States.

The first American flag raised in California was that which General Fremont raised on Fremont's Peak, overlooking the towns of Hollister and San Juan de Bautista, more generally known as San Juan South.

The copper used in the construction of the cruiser *Charleston* came from a Campo Seco, Calaveras County, mine.

Santa Barbara raises more pampas-grass plumes than any other place in the United States.

Vina vineyard contains 3,500,000 vines.

The longest lumber flume in the State is in Madera County, extending from above Fresno Flats to Madera, and it is sixty miles long.

Fresno County produces over one-half the raisin crop of the State.

San Francisco never had but one genuine snowstorm in the memory of any one living, and that occurred December 31, 1882, when the snow fell about three inches deep and remained on the ground twenty-four hours.

The first pig tin ever produced in the United States was from the Temescal mines, and consisted of 207 pigs, or 12,000 pounds.

The first railroad constructed in this State was in 1854, from Sacramento to Folsom, twenty-two miles.

The first street car cable line ever constructed was on Clay street, San Francisco.

The Sacramento is the longest river in the State, being 400 miles from its source in Goose Lake. The San Joaquin is 350 miles; Klamath, 275 miles, Feather, 250 miles; Kern, 125 miles.

The largest cantilever bridge in the United States is at The Needles, San Bernardino County, over the Colorado River. Its length of span is 360 feet.

Fresno has produced a sweet potato weighing 44¾ pounds.

Sacramento is the largest producer of hops of any county in the United States.

The first shipment of wines to France was in 1891, from Napa County, consisting of 800 puncheons.

English wine merchants now send special buyers to California to supply their cellars.

The first raisins marketed in this State were from Marseilles Valley, Butte County, in 1864. The first carload sent East was by J. P. Whitney, of Rocklin, Placer County, in 1874.

The Mariposa Big Tree Grove has 427 big trees. The largest is thirty-four feet in diameter. Through a tunnel or hole cut in one a four-horse stage is driven daily.

San Francisco has more miles of cable street car lines than any other city in the world. About 120 miles are in operation.

The largest sequoia tree in circumference is in Tulare County, given by United States surveyors at 109 feet. The tallest is the "Keystone," in Calaveras, being 365 feet high.

The first olive trees planted in this State were at San Diego, in 1769. They are still producing fruit.

The largest Irish potato reported last year was from San Luis Obispo County. It was forty-six inches long and weighed thirteen pounds.

The tallest cornstalk ever reported was raised near Anaheim, Los Angeles County. It was thirty-six feet high.

The oldest flouring mill now running is at Valley Ford, Sonoma County. It was started in 1853.

The oldest settlement in the northern part of the State was by the Russians, who built Fort Ross, Sonoma County, in 1811.

The only antimony mines in operation in America are in San Benito County.

It is claimed that Sierra has produced more gold than any other county in the State.

Kern County has the most extensive system of irrigating canals under one ownership in the United States. The largest canal is 32 miles long, 100 feet wide, banks 8 feet high, with 65 distributing ditches 150 miles long.

The first printing press used in California was at Monterey in 1834.

The largest flouring mill in the State is at Crockett, Contra Costa County, with a capacity of 6,000 barrels a day.

Forestville, Sonoma County, has a chair factory now in operation which was established thirty-seven years ago, and has made over half a million chairs.

California is the only country using the combined harvesters run by a traction engine, cutting a swathe forty feet wide, and threshing and sacking grain as it proceeds.

San Bernardino produces more oranges than any other county in the United States.

San Bernardino is the largest county in the United States, covering 21,172 square miles.

San Diego leads every county in the United States in the production of honey. One bee-owner has 6,000 hives.

The only buhach (pyrethrum) plantation in America is located near Atwater, Merced County, consisting of 300 acres.

Ventura County is the largest producer of Lima beans in the world.

Tehama County raises 1,000,000 pounds of peanuts annually.

Bakersfield, Kern County, has produced an orange clingstone peach measuring fourteen inches in circumference and weighing twenty-three ounces.

Sacramento is the largest shipper of green fruits, hops and vegetables of any point in the State.

San Juan Capistrano, Orange County, raised a water-melon weighing 150 pounds, and measuring five feet six inches in length and four feet nine inches in circumference.

The first religious services held in this State was on June 17, 1579, near Point Reyes, Marin County, by Sir Francis Drake's chaplain.

Stockton's Courthouse is the only one in the United States that is lighted and warmed by natural gas from its own gas well, and also supplied with artesian water.

The largest money check ever drawn in the United States was one for $10,000,000 on the Bank of Nevada.

The oldest paper mill in the State is at Taylorville, Marin County. It was established in 1853, and is still in operation.

The average annual income of every farmer in Sutter County is about $3,000, and the averaged assessed property is about $2,000 to each voter.

Inyo County has credit for producing two-thirds of the total silver product of the State.

Near Templeton, San Luis Obispo County, is the largest bearing prune orchard in America of 22,000 trees.

The oldest water-power sawmill is in Mill Valley, Marin County. It was erected in 1834 and is now standing.

Santa Clara has more acres in fruits and vines than any other county in the State.

The largest orange tree in the State is at Campo Seco, Calaveras County, and it is now 33 years old. Its oranges often take premium at fairs.

The largest nugget of gold ever found in the United States was at Carson Hill, Calaveras County, November, 1851. It weighed 195 pounds Troy and was valued at $43,534.

Stockton is the largest manufacturing city outside of San Francisco, and the factories are run by natural gas from gas wells costing from $2,000 to $10,000.

At Cave City, Calaveras County, is found one of those peculiar habitations used by primitive man in which are the mouldering bones of unknown ages.

Sonoma has more grape-vines and pear trees than any other county in California.

The most extensive oil pipe-line system in the West is from the Ventura Oil Works, 170 miles long.

The largest fig tree in California, measuring over eleven feet in circumference, is growing near Burson, Calaveras County, and annually produces large crops.

An English walnut tree at Vallecito, Calaveras County, measures nine feet in circumference and is probably the largest in the State.

CALIFORNIA—LAND OF THE GOLDEN SUNSET 21

The only malt whisky manufactory in the United States is at Sausalito, Marin County, according to Government reports.

The first quartz mill was erected in Grass Valley in 1850. Since then the quartz mills of Nevada County have produced over $100,000,000.

The largest cork oak tree of California is growing at Campo Seco, Calaveras County, and measures seven feet eleven inches in circumference.

The largest cherry tree in the State is near Newcastle, Placer County. It annually produces over $200 worth of early cherries.

Resorts and Springs—

Almost every visitor is interested in knowing how to reach the different health and pleasure resorts in the State, conveniently situated to San Francisco. The following is a list of the best-known resorts and medicinal springs, the route to be taken to reach them, distance from San Francisco by rail and stage, and the cost of reaching them:

Ætna Hot Springs; Napa Valley, railroad to St. Helena, 64 miles, stage 15 miles, $4.05.

Angwin; Howell Mountain, Napa Valley, railroad to St. Helena, stage 8 miles, $3.05.

Auburn; Ogden route, rail 126 miles, $4.10, $3.60.

Bartlett Springs; Napa Valley route to Calistoga, 73 miles, stage 70 miles, fare $7.30; or by San Francisco & North Pacific Railroad to Hopland, 99 miles, stage 42 miles, $8.00.

Big Trees, Calaveras; Stockton, Milton and Merced train to Milton, 133 miles, stage 49 miles, $18.00.

Big Trees, Mariposa; Los Angeles train to Berenda, thence to Raymond, 199 miles, stage 40 miles, $12.00.

Big Trees, Santa Cruz; South Pacific Coast narrow gauge, 74 miles, $2.55.

Byron Hot Springs; Stockton train to Byron, 68 miles, stage 2 miles, $2.40.

Castle Crags; Oregon line to Castle Crags, 294 miles, $9.90.

Cazadero; North Pacific Coast narrow gauge, 87 miles, $2.50; round trip $3.75.

Congress Springs; South Pacific Coast narrow gauge to Los Gatos, 55 miles, stage 5 miles, $2.35.

Coronado Beach; Pacific Coast Steamship Company's steamer, 484 miles, $15.00; Southern Pacific Company's San Diego train, 611 miles, $20.00.

Del Monte; Southern Pacific, 4th and Townsend Street station, to Del Monte, 124 miles, $3.00.

Donner Lake; Ogden train to Truckee, 209 miles, stage 2 miles, $8.55.

Geysers; San Francisco & North Pacific to Cloverdale, 84 miles, stage 16 miles round trip, $8.50; or Napa Valley route to

Calistoga (summer only), 73 miles, stage 27 miles, round trip $8.50; in one way, out the other, $12.50 (summer only).

- Gilroy Hot Springs; Southern Pacific, 4th and Townsend Street station, to Gilroy, 80 miles, stage 10 miles, $3.70.

Glenwood Springs; South Pacific Coast narrow gauge to Glenwood, 66 miles, stage 4 miles, $3.60; round trip $6.60.

Highland Springs; San Francisco and North Pacific to Pieta, 92 miles, stage 15 miles, $4.50; round trip $8.00.

Kellogg's; Napa Valley route to Calistoga, 73 miles, stage 7 miles, $3.05.

Klamath Hot Springs; Oregon train to Ager, 362 miles, stage 20 miles, $15.00.

Lake Tahoe; Ogden train to Truckee, 200 miles, stage 14 miles, $9.30, $10.30; round trip $16.00.

Lick Observatory; South Pacific Coast narrow gauge, from ferry, or Southern Pacific Company broad gauge, from 4th and Townsend, to San Jose, 50 miles, stage 28 miles, $6.75 round trip.

Litton Springs; San Francisco & North Pacific to Litton Springs, 70 miles, $2.40; round trip $3.60.

Lower Soda Springs, see Castle Crags.

Madrone Springs; Southern Pacific Company's Monterey train, 4th and Townsend, to Madrone, 69 miles, stage 14 miles, $3.35.

Mark West Springs; San Francisco & North Pacific to Santa Rosa, 51 miles, stage 9 miles, $2.50.

Mount Shasta; Oregon train to Sisson, 338 miles, $10.65; guide and horses to summit.

Napa Soda Springs; Napa Valley train to Napa, 46 miles, stage 5 miles, $1.50; round trip, limited, $3.50.

Pacific Congress Springs; Southern Pacific Company, 4th and Townsend, to Santa Clara, 47 miles, stage 11 miles, $2.25; or South Pacific Coast narrow gauge, from ferry, to Los Gatos, 55 miles, stage 5 miles, $2.15; round trip $4.25.

Pacific Grove; Monterey train, 4th and Townsend, to Pacific Grove, 128 miles, $3.25; Saturday to Monday round trip $5.25.

Palermo Orange Groves; Marysville and Oroville train to Palermo, 143 miles, $5.90.

Palo Alto, see Stanford University.

Paraiso Springs; Southern Pacific Company, 4th and Townsend, to Soledad, 143 miles, stage 7 miles, $4.75; round trip $9.00.

Paso Robles; Southern Pacific Company's Coast Division, 4th and Townsend, 216 miles, $6.20.

Redondo Beach; Southern Pacific Company's Los Angeles train, 505 miles, $15.50.

Sacramento (State Capital); Sacramento train at ferry, 90 miles, $1.50 (P. M. train only), $2.50, $3.30; by river steamer, 120 miles, $1.50.

San Jose; South Pacific Coast at ferry, or Southern Pacific Company at 4th and Townsend, 50 miles, $1.25; round trip Sunday $1.50.

Santa Clara, South Pacific Coast at ferry, or Southern Pacific Company at 4th and Townsend, 50 miles, $1.25; round trip Sunday, $1.50.

San Rafael, North Pacific Coast via Sausalito, or San Francisco & North Pacific via Tiburon, 15 miles; 35 cents, round trip 50 cents.

Seigler Springs, Napa Valley line to Calistoga, 73 miles, stage 34 miles, $6.00.

Skaggs Springs; San Francisco & North Pacific to Geyserville, 80 miles, stage 8 miles, $3.50; round trip $5.50.

Tuscan Springs; Oregon line to Red Bluff, 199 miles, stage 7 miles, $7.45.

Upper Soda Springs, Oregon line to Upper Soda Springs, 299 miles, $10.10.

Vacaville; Ogden line to Elmira, to Vacaville, 65 miles, $2.30, $2.05.

Vichy Springs; San Francisco & North Pacific to Ukiah, 113 miles, stage 3 miles, $4.75.

Wawona; Los Angeles train to Raymond via Berenda, 199 miles, stage 38 miles, $11.00.

White Sulphur Springs; Napa Valley line to St. Helena, 64 miles, stage 2 miles, $2.30.

Yosemite Valley; via Milton, 121 miles, stage 85 miles, round trip $40.00; via Raymond, 199 miles, stage 60 miles, round trip $50.00. Two other stage routes lead into the valley, one via Priests and the Tuolumne Grove of Big Trees, stage 85 miles, round trip $40.00; and the other via Calaveras Big Trees, stage 140 miles, round trip $50.00.

SAN FRANCISCO:

The Imperial City by the Western Sea.

※

The Gates of the City—

Whoever would visit the California Midwinter Fair must first enter the gates of the Imperial City by the western sea which like ancient Rome, sits supremely on a throne of hills. Barely forty-five years old, San Francisco now has a population of over three hundred thousand inhabitants and, in addition to being the commercial metropolis of the Pacific Coast, stands in the front rank of the great cities of the nation as the eighth on the list. It occupies the extremity of a peninsula, covering twelve square miles, and is flanked by one of the finest bays in the world on the one side and by the waters of the Pacific Ocean on the other.

The Golden Gate—

The visitor who would enter this city from the sea must pass through a narrow gorge intersecting the outer Coast Range and known as the Golden Gate. This entrance is not over a mile wide at its narrowest point. On the south side rises an irregular wall capped with shifting sand dunes, beyond which lies the city and the site of the Midwinter Fair; on the north, the bold and frowning cliffs of Marin County rise abruptly from the water's edge and are surmounted by the towering peak of Mt. Tamalpais. For the guidance of mariners, a light-house has been placed by the United States government on the Farallone Islands, a group of barren rocks of volcanic origin standing in the open sea thirty-five miles west of the Gate. Another light is stationed on the north head of the entrance—Point Bonita—and still others on Forts Point and Alcatraz, inside the harbor. The depth of water in the Gate is great enough to permit the largest vessel afloat to pass with safety at any stage of the tide. The government has strongly fortified it with batteries of heavy guns, some of which are situated on the crown of the southern wall; others have been erected at Lime and Fort Points, within the Gate, and still others on Angel and Alcatraz Islands which command the entrance within the bay.

It is through this ocean gateway that the commerce of the nation with the Orient, with the islands of the Pacific, with Australasia, the Russian Asiatic Possessions, British Columbia, the western coasts of South and Central America and the bulk of the commerce of Mexico passes; but no unfriendly ship can make the passage without first running the gauntlet of the bristling batteries which serve as its guardians.

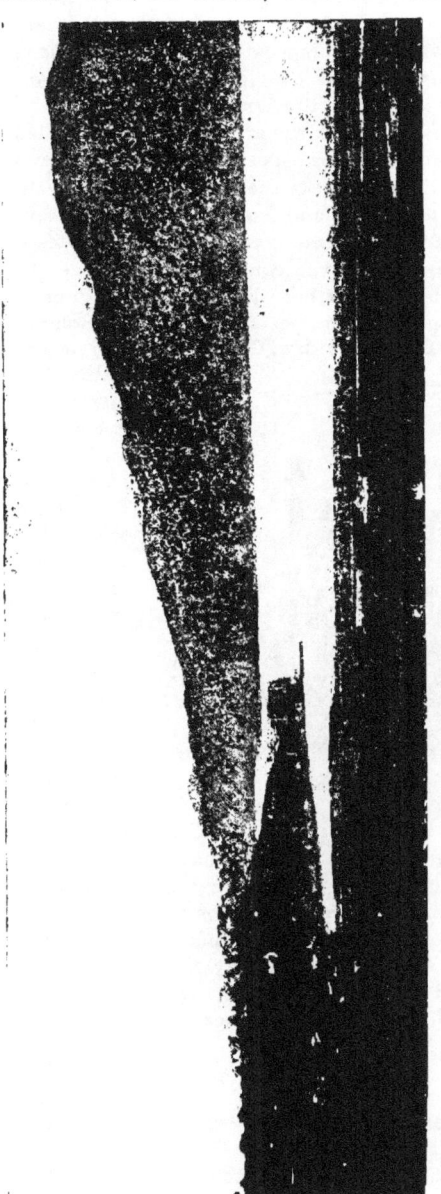

GOLDEN GATE, FROM PACIFIC HEIGHTS

The Eastern Entrance—

The eastern entrance to the city is trans-bay. The Eastern visitor who makes the trip to the Midwinter Exposition by rail must come in this way, no matter whether the southern, central or northern transcontinental route is followed. As all roads led to Rome in the days of its greatest glory, so all transcontinental railroads, whether on Canadian or American soil, so far constructed, make San Francisco their western terminus, car and ferry boat connecting on the Eastern shore of the bay.

The Largest Ferry Boat in the World—

All routes by land practically converge at Port Costa, situate at the northern end of Carquinez Strait which for many years past has been the chief wheat shipping point in the State. It is also the southern landing place of the ferry steamer *Solano*, which has the distinction of being the largest ferry boat in the world, its deck room being equal to the area of one acre. This mammoth steamer is used for the transportation of trains across Carquinez Strait between Benicia (once the State Capital), situate on the north side of the waterway, and Port Costa. All passengers by rail by the northern and central railroad routes— namely: by the Canadian Pacific, who continue their journey to San Francisco by land; by the Northern Pacific and the Central Pacific—make the passage of Carquinez Strait on the Solano. The boat is, in reality, a floating bridge, driven by steam, as the trains are carried on it bodily over the straits.

DECK OF LARGEST FERRY BOAT IN THE WORLD

The time occupied in making the passage affords the tourist an opportunity to inspect one of the most remarkable marine structures in existence and to "take in" one of the most interesting water and land scapes he has probably ever viewed. Mare Island, the United States Navy Yard, stands to the west; the city of Benicia spreads out over the hills on the north, and Martinez and Port Costa nestle under the lee of the Contra Costa hills on the south, while midway flows the current of the San Joaquin and Sacramento rivers, dotted with bay and river craft, engaged in commerce or in pleasure.

Bay Ferries—

Passengers by the Santa Fé and Southern Pacific railroads do not cross Carquinez Strait but they join the drift of railroad travel to San Francisco at Port Costa. An hour's ride from Port Costa brings the eastern, northern and southern trains into the great ferry building at the end of Oakland mole, which is practically the terminal point of the transcontinental railroad system. There, all passengers are transferred to the ferry boat in waiting. The steamers employed on the Oakland and San Francisco ferry are the finest ferry boats in existence, being luxuriously furnished and equipped for the comfort of passengers. These ferry boats run between the two cities every half hour, making the passage across the bay—a distance of three and one-half miles—in from sixteen to eighteen minutes. From twenty-five to thirty thousand passengers are carried on these boats daily, at a cost of ten cents each way, for local fares. Similar ferry boats to those employed in the Oakland service also ply between San Francisco and Sausalito and Tiburon, Sausalito being the terminus of the North Pacific Coast Railway, a narrow gauge road, running into the northern redwoods and passing through a region of surpassing picturesqueness, and Tiburon being the terminus of the San Francisco and North Pacific Railroad, which traverses the beautiful Russian River Valley, as far north as the town of Ukiah, a region full of attractions to the tourist.

A BAY FERRY BOAT

Another line of ferry boats, similarly equipped, ply to and from Oakland by way of San Antonio Creek, which is a notable waterway to the tourist as it is the scene of the most important harbor improvement thus far undertaken by the United States Government on the Pacific Coast. And, still another ferry line joins the city with Alameda, the sister city of Oakland on the eastern shore of the bay. This constitutes the terminal of the South Pacific Coast Railway, a narrow gauge road running south along the eastern shore of the bay, through the pretty towns of Santa Clara and San Jose, thence to Los Gatos, which is attaining fame for its fine wines, where it enters the Santa Cruz Mountains, a wild and romantic range lying between the fertile Santa Clara Valley and the sea, emerging, finally, on the shore of Monterey Bay, at the old mission town of Santa Cruz, which is now a popular seaside resort.

The Metropolitan Artery—

All the bay ferries converge at or adjacent to the foot of Market Street, which almost bisects the city, and is in fact the main arterial thoroughfare of the metropolis. The streets joining this thoroughfare on the south, as far west as the base of the western amphitheater of hills shielding the city from the ocean— that is, to the junction of Valencia Street—run southerly at right angles with it. All the streets on the north side have been laid

THE NEW CALIFORNIA

out at right angles with one another, but at acute and obtuse angles with Market Street. The streets on the north of Market street, beginning at the waterfront, going westward, are (running nearly north and south) in their regular order as follows: East, Drumm, Davis, Front, Battery, Sansome, Montgomery, Kearny, Dupont, Stockton, Powell, Mason, Taylor, Jones, Leavenworth, Hyde, Larkin, Polk, Van Ness, Franklin, Gough, Octavia, Laguna, Buchanan, Webster, Fillmore, Steiner, Pierce, Scott,

Devisadero, Broderick, Baker, Lyon, Cemetery or Central Avenue, Walnut, Laurel, Locust, Spruce and Cherry Streets; and then the avenues: First, Second, Third and so on to Forty-ninth at the ocean beach.

Those running out of Market on the north side of it in nearly a due east and west course are, beginning at the ferries: Sacramento, California, Pine, Bush, Sutter, Post, Geary, O'Farrell, Ellis, Eddy, Turk, Tyler or Golden Gate Avenue, McAllister,

MARKET STREET AT POST STREET

Fulton, Grove, Hayes, Fell, Oak, Page, Haight, Waller, Kate, Ridley.

The streets at right angles to Market and on the south side of it, beginning at the waterfront, are as follows: East, Steuart, Spear, Main, Beale, Fremont, First, Second, Third, Fourth and so on out to Eleventh. At the last named street Valencia joins Market at an obtuse angle, and thenceforward the numbered thoroughfares intersect Valencia at right angles until Thirtieth Street is reached.

Notable Buildings—

The principal hotels and the finest business blocks in the city are located on either side of Market Street, and on the principal side streets immediately adjacent to it. Among those which are

MILLS BUILDING AND SURROUNDINGS

sure to rivet the attention of the tourist as he proceeds uptown from the ferry landings are the Luning Block, a new structure of quaint architectural design, occupying the California Street gore, the Grand and Palace Hotels, between Second and Third Streets, the latter the largest caravansary in the world and capable of accommodating 1200 guests; immediately opposite, on the Post Street gore, is the Crocker Block, built of Rocklin granite, Roman brick and terra cotta, and under its shadow, on the north side of

A MODEL BANK BUILDING

Post Street, stands the Masonic Temple. From this point may be seen also, when looking north along Montgomery Street, the Mills Building, constructed of Inyo marble and Roman brick with terra cotta ornamentations, while a massive structure of Raymond granite is being erected at the corner of Post and Montgomery, opposite the Masonic Temple. At the junction of Kearny, Market and Geary stands the Chronicle Building, a massive brick and Sespe (Ventura County) sandstone of a dark lavender color, crowned with a tall, turreted bronze clock tower, all constituting a splendid monument of the energy and enterprise and courage of the man who gave being to the Midwinter Fair, M. H. de Young, the proprietor of the *Chronicle*, and the Director General of the Exposition. On the south side of Market Street, directly opposite the Chronicle Building, is the Nucleus Block, the property of W. R. Hearst, the enterprising proprietor of the "monarch of the dailies," the *Examiner*, and which it is designed to reconstruct at a future day to serve as a suitable headquarters for that journal. The Phelan Block is a

MARKET STREET AT THE BALDWIN HOTEL

conspicuous building on the O'Farrell Street gore. The Flood Building, at the corner of Fourth and Market Streets, is a reminder of the great Comstock lode in its best days when the bonanza mines yielded their immense volumes of the precious metals for the enrichment of their owners, and adjoining it on either side are the Pioneer Building, with its frontage on Fourth Street, and the building of the Academy of Sciences, with its frontage on Market Street, monuments of the generosity of the late James Lick, who left the bulk of his great fortune as public benefactions. The Baldwin Hotel and Theater, at Powell and Market, the Odd Fellows Hall at Seventh and Market, the Murphy Block opposite, at the corner of Jones and Market, follow in quick succession as the tourist moves westward.

Natural Curiosities and Mineral Collections—

The Academy of Sciences is a magnificent structure, containing in the material employed in its erection specimens of all the many varieties of building stone to be found in this State and in the neighboring Territory of Arizona, including polished marble from Colton, pink sandstone from Arizona, lavender sandstone from Sespe, Ventura County, yellow sandstone from Gilroy, and granite, plain and polished, from various points in the State. The museum is worth the inspection of the visitor to San Francisco, for it contains a fine and rare collection of birds, animals, fishes, reptiles, shells and aboriginal implements, etc. It is free to the public.

The Pioneer Building is also the headquarters of the State Mining Bureau and contains in its museum a splendid collection of the minerals found in the State. An examination of the collection will give the visitor a suggestion, at least, of the great mineral wealth of California. Additions are being made continually to the collection, showing new developments in mining in every direction.

City and County Buildings—

Then comes the City Hall, occupying a three-cornered tract bounded by McAllister and Larkin Streets and Park Avenue. The site is historical, for the reason that it formerly constituted the cemetery ,,of Yerba Buena, where many of the pioneers who died in early days were buried. The remains were removed to Laurel Hill Cemetery in the latter sixties and earlier seventies to make way for the imposing pile of brick, stone and iron now standing on the spot. This structure has been over twenty years under construction and has cost nearly $4,000,000, but it is yet incomplete. It embraces a fire-proof building for the preservation of the municipal records, which is a circular structure, separate from the main building and connected with it by a corridor; all the city and county offices, the civil and superior criminal courts of the county, the rooms of the Supreme Court of the State, the Free and Law Libraries, police headquarters and a prison for the confinement of petty offenders and for the detention of those arrested for higher crimes until after their preliminary examination shall have been held. Other municipal buildings are the Old City Hall on Kearny Street, between Washington and Merchant; the County Jail, on Broadway, near Kearny; the Industrial School and Branch County Jail (formerly the House of

Correction), in the southwestern suburbs, and the Almshouse, on the western slope of the Mission Hills.

United States Buildings—

The United States has a Custom House and Postoffice, an Appraisers' Building, a Treasury Building and a Mint for the coinage of money.

United States Mint—

The United States Mint is the largest structure of that character in the country and is one of the handsomest public buildings in San Francisco. It fronts 161 feet on Mission and 217 feet on Fifth Street. It is built in the Doric style of architecture, with massive fluted columns at the entrance. The basement and steps are of California granite and the upper walls of freestone obtained from Newcastle Island, in the Gulf of Georgia. The machinery is of the latest pattern and is equal in efficiency to any used in the United States. When working to its full capacity the Mint can coin nearly 1,000,000 ounces per month. It contains one of the finest numismatic collections in existence, which is open to inspection by visitors, who are admitted daily between the hours of 9 A. M. and 12 M., and for whose special accommodation a conductor is provided by the Government to escort them through the building. It is easy of access by any of the Market Street and Mission Street cars direct or by transfer indirectly by any other line in the city. The building contains the offices of the Superintendent, Assayer, Coiner and all the attaches of their respective departments.

Custom House and Postoffice Block—

The Custom House and General Postoffice Building occupies the eastern half of the block bounded by Battery, Sansome, Washington and Jackson Streets. It is a somber three-story structure. The ground floor is occupied exclusively by the various departments of the General Postoffice, the main entrance being in the wing fronting on Washington Street. The upper two stories constitute the Custom House, the main entrance being on Battery Street. In the Custom House are quartered the Collector of the Port, the Surveyor of the Port, and the Naval Officer and the special agents of the U. S. Treasury Department with their respective subordinates.

The western half of the Custom House and Postoffice Block is occupied by the United States Appraisers' Building. It is a plain brick and stone edifice, four stories high, and contains besides the offices of the United States Appraiser, the rooms of the United States District and Circuit Courts, the offices of their respective clerks and commissioners, and the offices of the United

States Coast and Geodetic Survey. The main entrance to the U. S. Appraiser's Building is on the Sansome Street frontage; there are also side entrances, for public use, on the Washington and Jackson Streets frontages.

Cars of the Central, the Union Street and the Cliff House and Ferries Railroad Companies pass close by the Custom House, Post-office and Appraisers' Building.

Branch Postoffices

Branch Postoffices are located as follows.
Branch Postoffice A, 1309 Polk.
Branch Postoffice B, Mission and Eighth.
Branch Postoffice C, Mission and Twentieth.
Branch Postoffice D, foot of Market.

For the accommodation of visitors, a branch postoffice has also been established at the Fair grounds.

United States Branch Treasury—

The United States Branch Treasury is an unpretentious three-story brick and stone structure standing on the north side of Commercial Street, between Kearny and Montgomery Streets. Only the lower part of the building is used by the Assistant Treasurer of the United States for his offices, and in these quarters are located the big vaults in which the Federal Government's coin and securities are stored.

The upper floors are occupied by the United States Surveyor-General for California, and by the Registrar and Receiver of the United States Land Office.

Horse cars of the North Beach & Mission and the Third and Montgomery Street branch of the Omnibus Cable Co.'s lines, and the cable cars of the California Street and the Ferries and Presidio Co.'s lines, run convenient to the Treasury Building.

Other Interesting Institutions—

Shot Tower, First and Howard.
Merchants' Exchange, California below Montgomery.
Stock Exchange, Pine near Montgomery.
Wells, Fargo & Co.'s Express, New Montgomery and Jessie Streets.
Chinese Merchants' Exchange, 739 Sacramento.

Notable Residences—

Many private residences in the city are famous the world over. This is particularly the case with those crowning the summit of California Street Hill, popularly styled "Nob Hill," the most conspicuous elevation in the city. A ride of a few minutes from Market Street on the California Street cable cars, or from the ferry landing, by the more roundabout way of the Powell Street branch of the Ferries and Cliff House Railroad, brings the tourist to the scene of the costly structures erected by the late Mark Hopkins, Charles Crocker and Leland Stanford. The Stanford residence, which is occupied by the Senator's widow, is reputed to have cost $2,000,000; the Crocker residence, $2,500,000, and the Hopkins residence, which was the last of the three to be built, the enormous sum of $2,750,000. Each of these

THE STANFORD RESIDENCE

magnificent structures command a splendid view of the city, the bay and the territory surrounding it. They are also surrounded by elegant grounds, artistically laid out in lawns, flower beds and walks. The interiors of these houses have been fitted up with the costliest and rarest woods of the world's forests. The Hopkins mansion is now devoted to art, having been presented by

THE CROCKER RESIDENCE

Edward F. Searles, the surviving husband of the late Mrs. Mary Hopkins-Searles, to the San Francisco Art Association and the University of California, and it is under their joint control. On the block diagonally opposite the Hopkins Art Institute, fronting California Street, is the magnificent structure erected by the late James C. Flood, of bonanza fame, as a residence. It is built of

Connecticut brownstone, and is the only structure in the State built of that material. On the block farther west stands the residence of the late D. D. Colton, now the property of Collis P. Huntington, president of the Southern Pacific Company. The late Robert Sherwood erected the handsome residence standing opposite the Crocker residence, at the southwest corner of Cali-

MARK HOPKINS INSTITUTE OF ART

fornia and Taylor Streets. All of these buildings are historical for the reason that they are associated directly with the great fortunes that grew out of the construction of the Central Pacific Railroad and the wonderful mineral wealth of the great Comstock Lode in Nevada. If the visitor will take a trip along the Pacific Heights on the cars of the Ferries & Cliff House Cable Company's line he will see terraces of magnificent dwellings of a

THE FLOOD RESIDENCE

later production, besides enjoying one of the most attractive panoramic rides to be obtained on the street car service of the city, consisting of charming views of the city, glimpses of the bay and the Golden Gate, and a bird's-eye view of the harbor, its shipping and its islands, and the mountain terrace surrounding it and stretching through half a dozen counties.

Places of Amusement—

San Francisco is well provided with theatres and other places of amusement, at each of which popular plays are constantly presented.

A few years ago, the old California Theatre, for nearly a generation the leading playhouse of the city, on whose stage many of the leading stars of two continents appeared, was demolished and a finer and larger auditorium and a hotel erected on its site. The New California stands on Bush Street, between California and Dupont Streets. There is not a more richly appointed theatre in the country, while every attention for the comfort and safety of its patrons has been given in the arrangement of its interior and its exits.

The Alcazar is a smaller structure of rich Moorish design at 116 O'Farrell Street.

The Baldwin is a charming little theatre, rich in its furnishings and ornamentation, situated in the block at the northeast corner of Market and Powell Streets.

The Tivoli Opera House on Eddy near Powell always has a popular opera on the bill.

The Standard and Bush Street Theatres are on opposite sides of Bush Street, between Kearny and Montgomery Streets, and are devoted chiefly to light comedy.

The Grand Opera House is situated on Mission Street, west of Third. It is the largest theatre in the city and is capable of seating 2,500 persons, but it is not open regularly.

Other theatres are the Stockwell's, on Powell Street near Market; Chinese theatres, 626 and 623 Jackson and 814 and 836 Washington Streets.

Clubs—

Some of San Francisco's clubs are world-renowned, owing to the splendor of their quarters and the generous nature of their hospitality to distinguished visitors. The oldest club is the Union-Pacific—a combination of two organizations—which occupies magnificent quarters at the corner of Post and Stockton. The Cosmos Club is a near neighbor on Powell Street, fronting the same public park—Union Square, while near by—on Post Street near Grant Avenue—are the quarters of the Bohemian Club, which it now having a magnificent building erected on Sutter Street for its special use. Journalism is also represented in the Press Club, which has charming quarters and a large and influential membership. The Olympic Club, famed in athletics, is the leading organization devoted to athletics and out-door sports, and it has fine grounds on the south side of Golden Gate Park, adjacent to the Midwinter Fair grounds. Almost every nationality in the community is also represented by a club, usually of a social and beneficiary nature.

Churches—

All denominations and creeds are represented in the religious institutions of San Francisco. Among them are many notable and costly structures. The largest of all is St. Ignatius Church, which, with the Jesuit College adjoining it, constitutes one of the most imposing groups of buildings in the city. It occupies the block bounded by Van Ness Avenue, Franklin, Grove and Hayes Streets. The church will accommodate six thousand persons. The spires stand 275 feet above the ground, and are the highest in the State. Other notable churches belonging to the Roman Catholics are: St. Mary's Cathedral, also on Van Ness Avenue, at the corner of O'Farrell Street; St. Patrick's Church, which possesses a full chime of bells, located on Mission near Third. Another imposing structure is Temple Emanu-El, on Sutter Street near Powell, a Jewish synagogue. The Unitarian church on Geary and Franklin Streets is the direct successor of the famous Starr King's church, which, in its day, occupied a site on Geary Street near Stockton, now occupied by business blocks. Congregationalists, Presbyterians, Episcopalians, and other denominations have also many fine and costly edifices.

Public Libraries—

San Francisco contains six libraries. These have an aggregate of two hundred thousand volumes on their shelves. The Free and Law Libraries are in the west end of the City Hall. The Mercantile Library is on Van Ness Avenue, corner of Golden Gate Avenue. The Mechanics' Library is on Post Street, between Montgomery and Kearny. The others are the San Francisco Verein and the French Libraries.

Art Association—

The San Francisco Art Association's gallery is in the Hopkins Art Institute on California Street, at the corner of Mason. It contains a fine collection of the best works of California artists.

Cemeteries—

San Francisco is provided with some of the finest cemeteries in existence. Laurel Hill, the burial place of dead pioneers; Calvary, the Roman Catholic burial ground; Odd Fellows' Cemetery and the Masonic Cemetery crown the fringe of hills lying between the city proper and Golden Gate Park, and the visitor to the latter will, no matter which way he enters, pass by these cities of the dead. Hills of Eternity, Holy Cross and Cypress Lawn lie across the southern boundary line of the city in San Mateo County, and Mountain View Cemetery nestles in the beautiful hills back of Oakland, across the bay.

SIDEWALK SCENE IN CHINATOWN

The Chinese Quarters—

The Chinese quarters in San Francisco are a source of never-failing interest to the visitor, for they furnish a means ready at hand to study orientalism in all its unique and peculiar features.

These "quarters" are located in the very heart of the city, surrounded on all sides either by the business establishments of the whites, or hemmed in by their habitations. On one side, "the quarters" are actually bounded by the premises of the wealthiest

INTERIOR CHINESE RESTAURANT

white denizens of San Francisco, and it is only a step, as it were, from the most repulsive of Oriental squalor, to the greatest of Caucasian luxuriousness. It is estimated that there are over 80,000 Chinese in the United States. Of this number nearly one-third are huddled together in the territory bounded on the north by Pacific Street, on the south by California Street, on the east by Kearny Street, and on the west by Mason Street, comprising not over twelve blocks. In some parts a labyrinth of passages intersects the district, constituting a maze impossible for the uninitiated to traverse with certainty or security, while the

CHINESE VEGETABLE VENDOR

ground underneath is honeycombed like a rabbit warren, these human burrows in some instances descending below the level of the sewers in their vicinity. No one ventures to explore the inner recesses of the Chinese quarters without being accompanied by an experienced guide. It is, of course, possible and safe to traverse the principal thoroughfares passing through "the quar-

AN OPIUM SMOKER

Copyrighted
Taber, S. F.

ters" without a guide; and there is much which the visitor can thus see that is curious, while glimpses may be obtained here and there of those vices and phases in their civilization which make association with the Mongolian race so repugnant to the average person of Caucasian blood. The Chinese joss-houses or temples for the worship of their deities; the Chinese theatres; the

Chinese restaurant, and even the Chinese vendor and artisan, who is encountered at almost every step in a tour through Chinatown, are each and all so different in kind and appointment to those of our own race that they become subjects of intense interest to those who have not seen them before. But the pungent fumes of burning opium which offend the nostrils every-

OPIUM DEN INTERIOR   Copyrighted Taber, S. F.

where throughout "the quarters," and an occasional glimpse which may be, now and again, obtained into some partially concealed interior, suggests the presence of the vice which the Asiatic has introduced into our midst, and which is thus undermining the morals and constitutions of many youths of our own race. The visitor may enter the sacred precincts of the Chinese

JOSS HOUSE INTERIOR   Copyrighted, 1887 Taber, S. F.

joss-houses or temples without fear of sacrilege. This intrusion among the sacred vessels of the temple and the material representations of the deities they worship, will be witnessed by the Chinese worshippers with stoical indifference. There are six principal joss-houses and a number of smaller temples in the city, but there is nothing about the exterior or interior to suggest the splendor of the pagan temples to be found in the Orient. The visitor to Chinatown will marvel at the great number of men

CLIFF HOUSE AND SEAL ROCKS

rushing hither and thither through "the quarters," and the almost total absence of women and children.

Holidays in Chinatown—

Sunday is a good day to see Chinatown in full blast. Its streets are then thronged by the men employed in the factories throughout the city. But the gala day of all holidays in the year is Chinese New Year, which begins with the first new moon after the sun has entered Aquarius, always occurring some time between January 21st and February 18th. The visitor to the Midwinter Fair who is fortunate enough to be in San Francisco during Chinese New Year will witness a scene never to be forgotten. A Chinese procession is also a wonderful spectacle, the pageant being unique in its barbarous splendor and display.

Seal Rocks, the Cliff House and Sutro Park—

Near the western or ocean extremity of Golden Gate Park stand the Seal Rocks, famous as the rookeries of these fur-bearing amphibians. They comprise a group of small, barren and wave-washed rocks, lashed by the heaving waters of the Pacific Ocean, outside the South Head to the Gate, Point Lobos. They are at all times interesting objects to visitors, for the reason that they offer an opportunity to inspect and study the animals occupying them in their native element. They are protected from slaughter by law, their molestation being strictly prohibited, as they constitute in foggy weather valuable aid to those mariners seeking to enter the Golden Gate, by means of the loud barking which they keep up incessantly, and which serves as a note of warning of their proximity to danger. When a storm is raging, these rocks present a grand spectacle, the great waves lashing their sides and deluging them with spray, the seals in great commotion seeking shelter to leeward and bellowing louder than the roll of thunder which follows the violent shock of wave and shore.

Towering above these seal rookeries, perched on the edge of the precipice forming at this point the shore line of the mainland, stands the famous hostelry of the Cliff House, and, on a terrace still higher, Sutro Park and Sutro Heights, the home of Adolph Sutro, the constructor of the great tunnel bearing his name, which drains a large section of the Comstock Lode. Sutro Park has been reclaimed from the desolate and shifting sand dunes, and is a standing illustration of what art, energy, foresight and money, intelligently utilized, can accomplish. The Park is private property, but the owner generously admits the public to inspect it at pleasure. Sutro Heights contains also a large collection of statuary, plaster casts of the famous works of art in the old world.

Military Reservations—

San Francisco, being a garrisoned city, contains several military reservations. The chief one is the Presidio, where the officers' quarters and the main part of the garrison are located, This reservation covers an area of 1500 acres of land on the northern side of the city, fronting on the Golden Gate for a distance of two miles on each side of Fort Point. The latter is a brick fortress, erected under the shadow of a bluff on a low point of rocks projecting into the Golden Gate at its narrowest point, which gives its guns the sweep of the entrance to the bay. Guns are also mounted *en barbette* along the bluff above, and directly opposite the fort, on the Marin County shore, are the water batteries of Lime Point. The reservation is all enclosed, but the military authorities have thrown it open to the public, and, what is of vastly greater benefit, constructed through it a splendid

PRESIDIO MILITARY RESERVATION

system of carriage drives, which the public are at liberty to use without challenge. Much of the reservation has also been planted with trees, and it promises to vie in time with Golden Gate Park as a public pleasure ground. From the summit of Presidio Hill, which is reached by the military roadways, one of the finest panoramic views on the continent is obtained when sea, bay and shore are free from fog and haze. On the southern side of Presidio Hill, and visible from some parts of Golden Gate Park, is the United States Marine Hospital.

Another military reservation is located at Point San Jose, better known as Black Point. This fort is reached by the Union Street cable road to Polk Street, thence along the line of Polk

Street north to the bay shore. The fort is supplied with three 15-inch Rodmans, weighing 25 tons each and capable of throwing a solid projectile of 450 pounds, or a shell of 432 pounds. Point San Jose is the residence of the Department Commander.

All of the principal islands in the bay have been reserved for military purposes.

The old Mission Church—

The old Mission Church, founded by the Franciscan friars on the 8th of October, 1776, and completed ten years later, is still standing at the corner of Dolores and Sixteenth Streets. It is the oldest building in San Francisco. The structure is built of adobe, the walls being three feet thick, resting on a foundation of undressed stone. Originally, the roof was covered with tiling,

OLD MISSION DOLORES

like that covering the Monterey County Building at the Midwinter Fair; but in the modern work of repair and restoration shingles have been substituted. The building is still used for worship. Adjoining it is the Mission Cemetery, which stopped receiving interments in 1858. It contains the grave of Don Luis Arguello, the first governor of Alta California under Mexican rule, and it also contains a strong reminder of vigilante days, in the fact that here lieth the dust of James P. Casey, the slayer of James King of William, who was hung for the crime by the Vigilance Committee of 1856.

San Francisco Bay and Surroundings—

San Francisco Bay consists really of three broad sheets of water almost entirely surrounded by land and joined by very narrow straits to one another. The main bay lies, of course, east of the city, stretching north to where the Marin County hills and a low tongue of land from the Contra Costa County shore nearly meet, leaving only a narrow waterway between them, in the center of which stand two rocky knobs known as the "Two Brothers," on one of which a lighthouse has been erected. It extends over forty miles to the south to San Jose. North of the "Brothers" the land again recedes, leaving a broad, circular basin, nearly thirty miles across, which is known as San Pablo Bay. This is again connected by the strip of water already referred to as Carquinez Strait, with Benicia and Martinez on either shore at the northern end, and Vallejo and Mare Island, and Vallejo Junction on either side at the south end. North

GUARDIANS OF THE GOLDEN GATE

of this again is the bay of Suisun, which receives the waters of the San Joaquin and Sacramento Rivers, whose confluence is at the upper end.

Standing upon either one of the eminences upon which the city is erected, a fine view of the main bay, or San Francisco Bay proper, and its surroundings is obtained. In the northern foreground stand the Marin County Hills, and, in the hazy distance beyond, the blue ranges of Sonoma and Napa Counties, which lie beyond San Pablo Bay. To the northeast and east the Contra Costa Hills sweep in a semi-circle behind the towns and cities and hamlets of Alameda County, consisting of Berkeley, the seat of the University of California; Oakland, the educational, center of the Pacific Coast; Alameda, a charming suburban city; San Leandro, San Lorenzo, Haywards, Niles and other towns famous for their orchards and vineyards. In the middle distance, looking in that direction, are the bay islands, their rounded domes and green slopes contrasting harmoniously with the gray waters of the bay. These islands consist of Alcatraz, which is a strongly fortified rock and is also used as a military prison; Angel Island, which is also fortified on the northwestern extremity and is the site of the quarantine station; and Goat or Yerba Buena Island, which lies immediately in front of the city and almost in the track of the Oakland ferries. This is now used by the United States Government as a station for lighthouse supplies, the wharf and buildings of which may be seen in crossing the bay in the little cove on the eastern side; and also as a torpedo station, with a squatty, one-story, fire-proof structure, built for the purpose under the lee of a headland on the northeastern end of the island. This island is capable of being strongly fortified, but so far no forts have been established on it. It was formerly used as a military post, but buildings and troops were moved many years ago to the Presidio, a large military reservation situated on the north end of the city. To the south, the bay dissolves in the hazy distance, and the eye looking to the west rests on Bernal Heights and the Mission Peaks, overlooking the busy city below.

San Francisco at Night—

The city at night is an interesting sight, whether seen from the summit of the hills or from the decks of the bay ferry boats. It is a blaze of light, in either case, thrown out from parallel lines of burning electric and gas lamps, climbing up the sides and over the summits of the hills, spreading over the low Mission flats and stretching like strings of brilliants along the docks and wharves on the waterfront. On clear weather, its twinkling lights can be made out thirty or forty miles off at sea and quite as far inland.

Neighboring Towns—

A trip of half an hour, by either of their respective ferry boats, will take the visitor across the bay to Oakland, a city of over 50,000 inhabitants, the largest of San Francisco's neighbors and a beautiful city of homes; or to Alameda, its nearest neighbor on the south, with a population of about 12,000; or to Berkeley, Oakland's northern neighbor, the home of the University of California, with a population of about 8,000; or to Sausalito and Tiburon. An hour's ride by rail takes the visitor to the beautiful cities of Santa Clara and San Jose, at the south end of the bay; or the same time by rail and water carries one to San Rafael, the charming county seat of Marin, while Napa, the Soldiers' Home, St. Helena and Calistoga may be reached in three hours.

The Grandest Drive in America—

Any visitor to San Francisco, desiring to enjoy one of the finest all-day drives on the continent, and having the means to procure a suitable team, can have his desire gratified within the limits of this city. Say, then, that the start is made at the junction of Golden Gate Avenue, the main thoroughfare leading to the Park, and Market Street. Reaching Van Ness Avenue, a turn is made north and that fashionable thoroughfare is followed to any one of the streets at the north end leading to the Presidio Reservation. Then let the driveway on the reservation, leading by the Barracks, Fort Point and over the Presidio Hill, be followed to the southern side of the reservation, where a good drive is to be obtained across the comparatively open stretch to the south to Golden Gate Park. Once there, the drives of the Park may be followed in a direct or roundabout way, as inclination may prompt, to the ocean beach; thence to the north up the side of the cliff to Point Lobos, the Cliff House, Sutro Aquarium and Baths, carved out of the cliffs, and Sutro Heights; thence, returning to the beach and following the shore past the United States Life Saving Station, a safe distance from the breaking surf, which will in time be made into a great highway, two hundred feet in width and elevated several feet above the level of high tide, until Ocean View House is reached. There, the beach is left in the rear and the horses' heads are turned to the east, toward the range of hills lying between the beach and the city beyond. Ascending the slope of the range, the Almshouse is passed on the left, and at the summit the road suddenly emerges through Mission Pass, a narrow gap in the range, and the great city bursts suddenly in view at one's feet, the bay and its islands, and the mainland beyond, studded with human habitations, all coming within the line of vision. From there it is an agreeable drive down the grade to Seventeenth Street, and at Dolores Street a deviation of one block to Sixteenth Street will take you past the oldest building in San Francisco, Mission Dolores, erected in 1776, 119 years ago, and the only reminder of the Mexican occupation of California now standing in the city. If time permits, the drive may be continued southeastward to South San Francisco, where the dry dock at Hunter's Point may be inspected; thence northward past the Potrero, where the Union Iron Works —the works of the Pacific Coast naval constructors—the Spreckles Sugar Refinery and the Pacific Rolling Mills are located. The Union Iron Works are famous as the builders of the *Charleston*, the *San Francisco* and the *Olympia*, cruisers; and the harbor defense ship *Monterey* and the battle ship *Oregon*. The water front may then be followed as near as the pleasure seeker desires to drive, returning to the point of beginning. It is an all-day drive, and will test the mettle of a good team; but it is one that will well repay the expense, time and trouble. It will be a day into which a greater variety of sights and scenery will have been crowded than can be compressed into a day's drive in any other part of America.

The Climate Around San Francisco Bay—

October is usually the warmest month in the year in San Francisco and around the bay. The mean temperature in July is 57°. An average year does not contain more than half a dozen days when the temperature is 80° or upwards. From April until the end of August the western trade winds prevail, accompanied with more or less fog, being strongest and coolest in the month of June. Through the rest of the year the winds are variable. The weather is agreeable, however, at all times of the year. Winter is practically unknown here, that is, as it is known in the Eastern and Central States. The temperature seldom drops below the frost line; snow is a very rare visitant. Lawns remain green the year round; tender semi-tropical plants, such as are raised only under cover in the East, grow and bloom in the open air here throughout the year. The Eastern visitor to the Midwinter Fair will have abundant convincing proof of this fact, for the beds and borders in Golden Gate Park are planted with delicate flowers and tender shrubs, which were in full bloom at the opening of the Exposition, and which never cease to yield their fragrant and beautiful tributes to the hand that cultivates them. Yet a very light frost would leave its blighting mark on any one of these should it settle upon them, telling the tale of low temperature quite as plainly as the recording marks of any thermometer. And these plants are neither sheltered by glass nor fostered by artificial heat. No doubt that thousands of those visiting the Midwinter Fair will behold for the first time in the Park grounds, in the gardens of San Francisco, Oakland and other cities around the bay, great masses of tender callas, roses in endless profusion, fuchsias laden with pendant drops, geraniums ablaze with blossoms, and magnolias scenting the air with globes of white at Christmas tide and through the winter months. To some people, the only disagreeable feature about San Francisco weather is the prevalence of sea fogs, which frequently envelop it in a dense and moist atmosphere. But the climate is, for all that, bracing and enervating, and the strong trade winds and ocean fogs are of great sanitary benefit. Persons desiring to escape from the presence of these ocean fogs and the harshness of the trade winds, can do so by merely crossing the bay to any of the suburban towns and cities, for neither winds nor fog penetrate very far inland, and both are very materially tempered by the time they reach the eastern shore of the bay.

Hotels and Boarding and Lodging Houses—

The city is well supplied with hotels furnishing first-class accommodations to guests, and with boarding houses and lodging establishments where patrons may enjoy ease and comfort. The principal hotels and boarding houses in town comprise the Palace, Grand, Occidental, Baldwin, California, Lick, Russ, American Exchange, Brooklyn, Pleasanton, Berkshire, Bella Vista, Windsor and others. A Midwinter Fair Hotel and Boarding Bureau has also been organized, through which the best quarters at the best rates

A TYPICAL FAMILY HOTEL

can be secured. This Bureau has been incorporated with a capital of $100,000. It is composed of well known and thoroughly responsible citizens, consisting of Will E. Fisher, of the well-known real estate firm of Will E. Fisher & Co., President; Eugene G. Davis, of Davis Bros., Golden Rule Bazaar, Vice-President; Henry Wadsworth, cashier Wells, Fargo & Co.'s Bank, Treasurer; Capt. C. B. Knocker, former general agent World's Fair Hotel Bureau, General Manager, and Chas. A. Sweetland, formerly assistant secretary World's Fair Hotel

Bureau, Secretary. This Bureau has carefully listed places where visitors to the Midwinter Fair can get the best of accommodations and fair dealing during their stay in the city. Its headquarters are at No. 14 Post Street.

Hack Fares—

Hack fares are regulated by ordinance, and every company furnishing hacks for hire can supply patrons with cards containing the official fares printed thereon. Every visitor to San Francisco, having occasion to employ a hack, should be informed on the official fares, for the average jehu is human and liable to err on the side which nets him the greater profit. Following is the schedule of fares fixed by the cab and carriage companies under the hack ordinances, within the district bounded by Broadway, Gough, and Twelfth Streets, and the City Front, or for one mile:

ONE-HORSE COUPÉ	HAND BAGGAGE FREE	TWO HORSE COUPÉ OR CARRIAGE
$1 00	One or two passengers	$ 1 50
	More than two passengers	2 00
25	Each additional mile (each passenger)	25
1 50	Calling and Shopping, first hour	2 00
1 00	Calling and Shopping, each subsequent hour	1 50
3 00	Theatres, Balls and Parties, both ways reserved	4 00
3 00	Weddings	4 00
2 00	German Hospital	2 50
2 00	City and County Hospital	2 50
2 50	St. Luke's Hospital	3 00
3 50	Funerals, three hours	4 00
	Funerals, over three hours, by the hour	
	Funerals—To City Cemetery	5 00
	Funerals—To Holy Cross Cemetery	6 00
2 50	Black Point	3 00
3 00	Oakland Point (ferriage extra)	4 00
4 00	Villa	5 00
4 00	Park Drive	5 00
5 00	Park Drive and to end of Beach Road	7 00
6 00	Ingleside, via Park	8 00
6 00	Cliff House, via Park and return	8 00
	Cliff House, via Park and return, via Ingleside	10 00
5 00	Races, Bay District Track	7 00
5 00	Alms House, via Park	7 00
3 00	Presidio	4 00
4 00	Presidio and Fort Point	5 00
5 00	Presidio and Fort Point Drive	6 00
7 00	Presidio, Fort Point and Park Drive	10 00
	Presidio, Fort Point, Cliff House and Park Drive	12 00
	14-Mile House	12 00

Detention after the time for which carriages and coupés are ordered will be charged by the hour.

Street Railroads—

The street railroads of San Francisco will be a novelty to most visitors from abroad, for the reason that they are operated chiefly by wire cables running underground, a method of furnishing motive power of California invention peculiarly suited to the topography of the site of the city. Latterly, all of the cable railroads in operation in San Francisco were consolidated under one general management. They all begin at or near the ferry landings at the foot of Market Street, and throw out their branches in every direction to the suburbs of the north, south and west. A uniform fare of five cents is charged on all lines, and, by a system of transfers in use, any point in the city can be reached, no matter what car may be first boarded by the passenger. The following is a directory of the various street railroads in the city and the lines to which transfers may be made without the payment of any additional fare:

California Street cars run from junction of California and Market Streets (one block from ferry) to cemeteries, and transfer to Hyde, from Hyde to Jones and Union Streets, and at Central Avenue to the motor line for the Park.

Ferries and Cliff House Railroad runs out Clay and Jackson Streets, from ferries to Central Avenue and California Streets; transfers to North Beach and Powell Street, and from Powell to all the Market Street lines and to Fifth Street; at Central Avenue to the Park motor line.

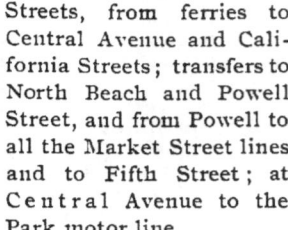

Geary Street, Park and Ocean Railroad runs from Geary and Market out Geary to Seventh Avenue and D Street. Transfers to North Beach and Mission cars, and at Market and Geary Streets to the ferries.

Market Street Cable Railroad runs cars from the ferries out Market to McAllister, Hayes, Castro, Valencia and Haight Streets. All the lines transfer to Geary, Powell, Fifth and Turk Streets. Transfers extra—the Hayes Street line (green cars) to Larkin Street cars, on eastward trips, and to Folsom Street, going south and west; the Castro Street (white cars) to Haight

Street line for the Park on eastward trips; Valencia Street (blue cars) same as Castro Street line, and also to electric cars for ferry on downward trips; Haight Street (red cars) to Valencia and Castro Street lines going west, on the eastward trips; Fifth Street cars transfer to electric cars, going both ways, and also to the Potrero.

The Omnibus Cable Company runs cable cars from ferry out Howard, and transfers to Third Street, Oak or Post Street, and Potrero Avenue cars; horse cars from ferries and transfers to Post, North Beach, Howard Street, and Brannan Street cars for Pacific Mail Dock; cable cars out Post, and transfers to North Beach, ferries, to Oak Street cars for Park on southward trips, and to Howard, Ellis and Potrero Avenue cars both ways. This system includes also the Oak and Ellis Street lines to the Park, the Brannan Street, South San Francisco and San Bruno lines.

The Sutter Street Railroad runs from the ferry out Sutter to Central Avenue. Transfers to Polk Street cars, both ways, and thence to Hayes, Mission, Folsom and Electric cars.

The Presidio and Ferries Railroad, or Union Street line, runs from ferries to Presidio. Transfers from Hyde for California Street cars and Park.

The San Francisco and San Mateo System runs electric motors to Ocean View and cemeteries (5 cents additional fare after crossing county line). Transfers to Potrero, Sixth, Mission, Valencia, and Larkin Street cars, through which the Park can be reached.

The motor lines for the Park and Cliff House (5 cents additional fare to the Cliff) start from Central Avenue and California Street. Transfers from Park to California and Jackson Street systems.

OPEN AIR PARK CONCERT IN MIDWINTER

GOLDEN GATE PARK:

Scene of the Midwinter Fair.

How to Reach It—

Golden Gate Park, the scene of the Midwinter International Exposition, lies on the western side of the city, beyond the outer terrace of hills. It has been for many years past a popular public resort, and all the street railroads in the city have, as a result, striven to get a share of the travel to and from it. Now, a system of transfers has been adopted by the various street railroad companies which enables one to travel to or from any part of the city and the Park on one fare. Conductors are always accommodating, and will impart such information as the unfamiliar passenger may desire so as to reach his or her destination.

What the Park Consists of—

The Park is an oblong tract of land fronting on the ocean beach for a distance of one half mile, and reaching eastward into the heart of the city at Stanyan Street—a distance of three miles. It embraces 1013 acres of land reserved by legislative enactment from the Pueblo lands of the city for park purposes, and it is under the control of a special Board of Park Commissioners, appointed by the Governor of the State. It is charmingly located. The broad expanse of the Pacific Ocean spreads out to the westward. South and east it is hemmed in by an amphitheatre of hills—the Mission Range, 925 feet in height, and Lone Mountain, 468 feet high; on the north, Presidio Heights, on the southern side of the Presidio military reservation, with Mt. Tamalpais looming up behind it from across the Golden Gate. Of late years, the city has stretched out toward it, and residences are crowding around it on all sides, dotting the green landscape of the hilly slopes with the evidences of human life and activity. Originally the entire tract was a cheerless, desolate waste of shifting sand-dunes, the surface of which was kept in constant motion by the sea breezes, and consequently was devoid of vegetation. Every foot of it had to be reclaimed, and the work of reclamation which was begun in 1874, has been so thoroughly done that it is now one of the finest, as it is one of the largest, public parks in existence. There are, in fact, only two larger public parks, owned by cities, in any part of the world, one being the Bois de Boulogne, near Paris, and the other Fairmount Park,

58 ALL ABOUT THE MIDWINTER FAIR

Philadelphia. In the improvement of Golden Gate Park there has been spent, up to date, about $1,000,000. Much of the land permanently reclaimed is in a high state of cultivation. It is divided artistically into grass lawns, flower beds, copses of beautiful shrubbery, groves of rare and valuable ornamental trees, ferneries, grottos, driveways and walks, everything being kept in the pink of order the year round. Acres of flower beds greet the eye on every hand, miles of flowering plants, in full bloom, follow the meanderings of the roadways; floricultural and arboricultural surprises confront the visitor whithersoever he roams through the grounds. A playground for children to make merry in has been provided through the benefaction of the Sharon estate, which is fitted with merry-go-rounds and other features of special interest to juveniles. There is also a well-stocked aviary; a deer park, in which herds of graceful animals find shelter; a buffalo paddock, with splendid specimens of the horned and bearded herd that once held sway over the American prairies—before railroads and Indians and tourists exterminated them; artificial lakes and fountains and waterfalls, suspen-

PARK SCENE AROUND GARFIELD MONUMENT

sion bridges, echo tunnels, baseball and cricket grounds, one of the finest conservatories in the country, which is stocked with a collection of the rarest tropical plants and orchids in existence,

THE SHARON PLAYGROUND FOR CHILDREN

a pond enclosed in it containing among other things a specimen of the gigantic Amazonian water lily, which will be in bloom during a great part of the Midwinter Fair, and which the visitor would look for in vain elsewhere outside of its native habitat and the Kew Gardens in London, whence the Park specimen was originally obtained. But what may interest the visitor from abroad more to know is, that with the exception of those features specially included within the enclosure of the Midwinter Exposition, the Park, as he sees it to-day, is in the same condition the year round. The lawns are always green; the flowering plants and shrubs are always in bloom; the calla lily unfolds its pure white chalice to the sunbeam of Christmas and New Year's Day as it does when the solar orb reaches the Tropic of Cancer in its yearly transit through the heavens, and the mignonette and the shy violet give forth their sweet fragrance with equal liberality here when the deep snows of winter cast a thick mantle over the Eastern visitor's home, and the Frost King locks its waterways in shackles of ice. And for many years past free open-air instrumental concerts have been given under the auspices of the Park Commissioners for the entertainment of visitors, by the best military band west of the Rocky Mountains. The music stand is a shell-shaped structure, and in the large open area fronting it seats have been provided for the accommodation of the auditors. These concerts are given every Thursday, Saturday and

THE CONSERVATORY

Sunday afternoons, rainy days excepted, of course, and thousands of persons attend them, by many of whom they are esteemed among the chief attractions of the Park. What better evidence of the geniality of San Francisco's climate can the visitor from abroad reasonably desire?

Entrances to the Park—

There are over twenty public entrances to Golden Gate Park, distributed on each side of the reservation. Most of them open into it on the eastern end, where the principal improve-

SUTRO HEIGHTS AND OCEAN BEACH

ments for public enjoyment and comfort have been made, and where the Fair grounds are located. All entrances, no matter where located, are reached by one or other of the street car lines.

Strawberry Hill—

The highest elevation in the Park, a conical hill, 426 feet high, called Strawberry Hill, is crowned with an observatory, from which is obtained a splendid view of the ocean, of the Park and the surrounding territory. A fine driveway leads to the summit of the hill, and the Observatory affords a welcome shelter to man and beast, once it is reached, from the chilling ocean breeze. On the summit of this hill also are located the Park water reservoir and girdling the base of the hill is a lake for boating, while cascades and other charming innovations crop out along its flanks. The Park is, of course, being enriched from year to year with costly works of art and monuments of distinguished men.

Halleck Monument—

A colossal figure in dark gray granite of General Henry W. Halleck, a California pioneer, and, from 1862 to 1864, General-in-Command of the United States Armies, stands in the center of a

INTERIOR OF PARK CONSERVATORY

green lawn, half enclosed by rising ground thickly set with trees and shrubbery adjacent to the Main Drive and midway between the Park Lodge and the Music Stand and Carriage Concourse. The secluded nook in which this statue stands is supplied with seats for the comfort of the wayfarer.

Garfield's Monument—

The bronze figure of the martyred President, James A. Garfield, is one of the most conspicuous of the Park monuments, occupying one of the most prominent places in it, and surrounded by the main drives. The figure of Garfield is ten feet high and it stands on a pedestal fourteen feet high. He is represented as he was when about to deliver his inaugural address on the steps of the Capitol at Washington. At the base of the pedestal Columbia sits mourning for her dead. The reliefs on the pedestal show Garfield taking the oath of office and other incidents in his career. The artist is F. Happersberger, a native of San Francisco.

Author of "The Star Spangled Banner"—

In memory of the author of the national hymn, "*The Star Spangled Banner*"—Francis Scott Key—a bronze statue by W. W. Story has been erected in Concert Valley, in front of the pres-

KEARNY STREET, LOOKING NORTH

ent music stand, as one of the bequests of the late James Lick, the founder of Lick Observatory, Lick Public Baths, Lick School of Mechanic Arts, and other public institutions.

The Baseball Pitcher—

Another statue of rare excellence is the bronze figure of the baseball pitcher, by a Californian deaf-mute. This work of art stands by the side of the north drive leading toward the Fair grounds. It has received the highest commendations of art critics.

Drake's Memorial Cross—

On the north side of Strawberry Hill is the monument erected under the auspices of the Episcopal Diocese of Northern California in commemoration of the first Christian service of record held on the Pacific shores of what is now the United States, namely the service held on the shore of Drake's Bay by Francis Fletcher, the chaplain of the flagship of Sir Francis Drake, when Drake landed there in 1579. The monument is a Celtic cross modeled on the lines of the ancient cross of Monasterboice, Ireland. The stem is richly carved after the manner of memorial edifices among the early Celtic Christians. The sub-base is seven feet, and the whole structure, which is made of Colorado sandstone, stands forty feet high. The following inscription appears on the front:

EPISCOPAL MEMORIAL CROSS

"Consecrated October 25, 1893, by the Church Missionary Council, as a memorial of the service held on the shore of Drake's Bay about St. John Baptist's Day, June 24, A. D. 1579, by Francis Fletcher, Priest of the Church of England, Chaplain of Sir Francis Drake, Chronicler of the Service."

The following legends are also inscribed on the other side of the shaft:

FIRST CHRISTIAN SERVICE OF KNOWN RECORD ON OUR COAST.

FIRST USE OF BOOK OF COMMON PRAYER IN OUR COUNTRY.

ONE OF THE FIRST RECORDED MISSIONARY PRAYERS ON OUR CONTINENT.

†

SOLI.
DEO.
SIT. SEMPER.
GLORIA.

†

The cross has been erected through the generosity of Geo. W. Childs, editor of the Philadelphia *Ledger*, who assumed the entire cost of the monument. In clear weather the site of Drake's Landing may be made out, under the shadow of Point Reyes, from the site of the cross.

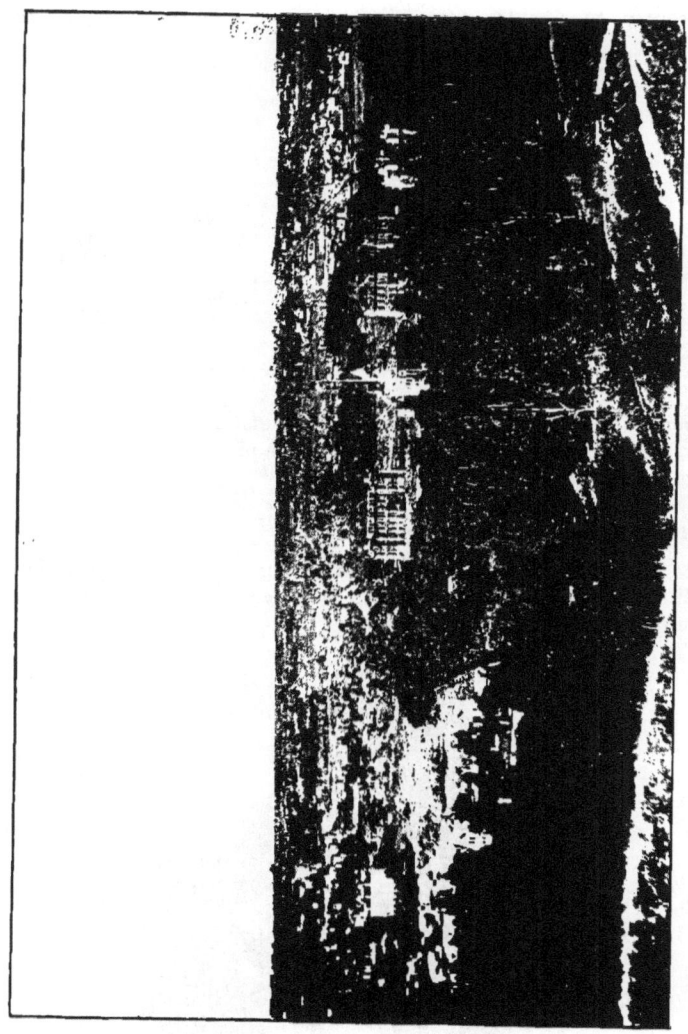

BERKELEY, LOOKING WEST

Respecting this memorial gift to California, Mrs. Mary Lynde Craig, editor of the Women's Department of the *Citrograph*, makes this appropriate comment on the unveiling of the cross: "Mr. Childs, whose kindly materialized thoughts apparently know neither financial nor geographical bounds, has on this New Year's Day linked the name of Sir Francis Drake, the great circumnavigator, with that of the printer-philanthropist of Philadelphia and the Midwinter Fair of San Francisco. Moreover, to us who have watched the progress of political events, it would seem a most fitting tribute to the sons of Colorado who have so recently, by popular vote, placed upon the head of woman in

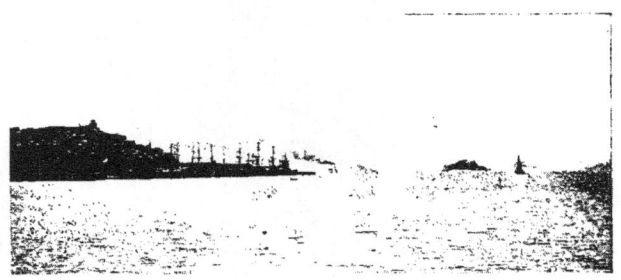

NORTH POINT, LOOKING TOWARD THE GATE

their commonwealth, the crown of the elective franchise. The prayer book cross, the Colorado crown and the Midwinter Fair, are this day linked together for all time."

Starr King's Monument—

A monument to Thomas Starr King, the patriot Unitarian Minister of *bellum* days, stands between the Aviary and the Buffalo Paddock.

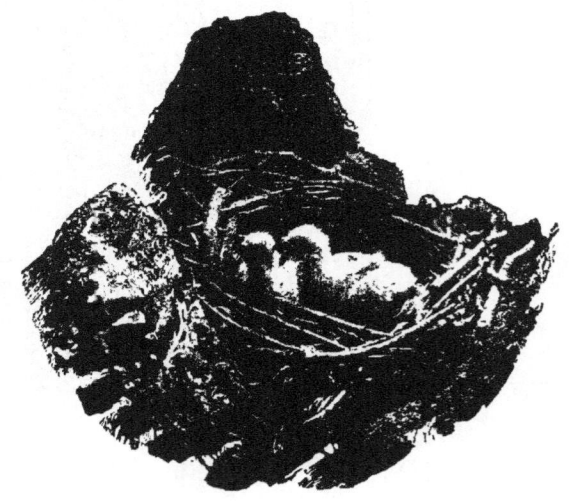

BIRD'S-EYE VIEW OF MIDWINTER FAIR

ADMINISTRATION BUILDING

California Midwinter International Exposition

★ ★ ★

Officers—

President and Director General	M. H. DE YOUNG
Vice-President	IRWIN C. STUMP
Asst. Director Gen. charge Foreign Affairs	R. CORNELY
Treasurer	P. N. LILIENTHAL
Executive Secretary	ALEXANDER BADLAM
Financial Secretary	JOHN HOESCH

PRESIDENT M. H. DE YOUNG

Executive Committee—

M. H. de Young, President, Irwin C. Stump, Vice-Pres.; Fulton G. Berry, J. S. Slauson, Eugene Gregory, A. Andrews, R. B. Mitchell, J. H. Neff, P. N. Lilienthal, Treasurer, Alexander Badlam, Secretary.

Exposition opened informally January 1, 1894.
Dedicatory Exercises and Permanent Opening, January 27, 1894.
Exposition closes June 30, 1894.

AGRICULTURAL AND HORTICULTURAL BUILDING

THE MIDWINTER FAIR:

In the Land of Flowers and Sunshine.

※

History of the Exposition—

The conception of the holding of an International Exposition in the middle of the winter season in any part of the temperate zone, was a bold one. The credit for it belongs unchallenged to M. H. de Young, proprietor of the San Francisco *Chronicle*, while a Director of the Columbian Exposition at Chicago; and its crystalization from a mere suggestion to a reality and from a nebulous condition to a tangible creation of life and order and substance has been due largely to his energy and untiring zeal, ably aided by a corps of co-workers, embraced in the Executive Committee, and a skillful staff of assistants to superintend the details of the various departments. Mr. de Young was very properly chosen the President and Director-General of the Exposition. There is no other part of the country, except California, where such an undertaking could have been attempted. The enterprise was broached on the 1st of June, and the visitor to the Midwinter Fair looks upon what has been planned, developed and executed in the short period of seven months. The site was not chosen until July 10th, and grading began August 29th. The first contracts for the Exposition buildings were awarded September 19th, and the beautiful city now by the Sunset sea has sprung into being in less time than three months out of the shapeless wilderness. The spirit that added the brightest star to the national galaxy, that opened the treasure vaults of nature to tide over the nation's needs in the hour of its direst extremity, and that furnished the courage and the ability to girdle the continent with an iron band over the Sierras and the Rockies and across the waterless deserts, is still living and California is its abode.

The Exposition Grounds—

The grounds occupied by the Exposition cover an area of 160 acres, lying between the north and south drives, and on either side of which stands the Buffalo Paddock, the Children's Playground, the Aviary and Strawberry Hill. The main buildings form a quadrangle. On the east side stands the Manufactures and Liberal Arts Building, of oriental design, 450 by 200 feet, built of wood, iron and glass, and covered externally with ornamental staff. Fronting it, on the west end of the quadrangle, is the handsome Administration Building, 60 by 40 feet, and having a dome 100 feet high, which is also constructed

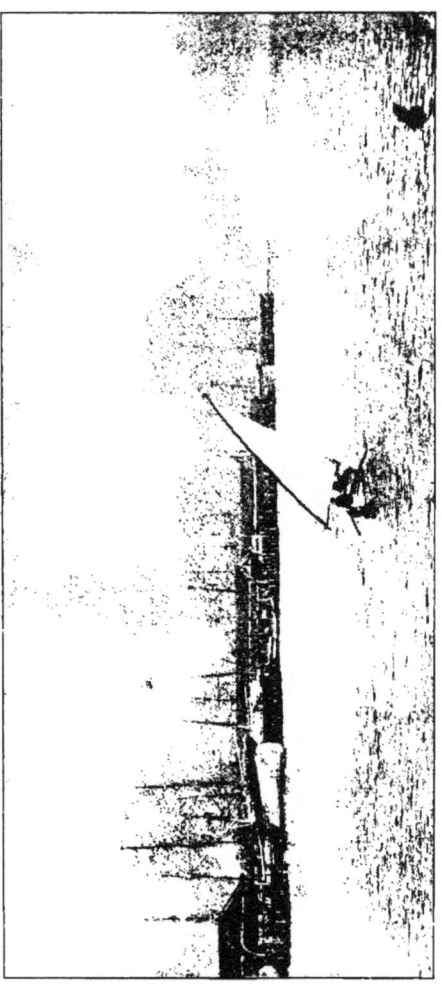

THE CITY FRONT, SAN FRANCISCO

of similar materials. On the south side of the quadrangle stands the Mechanical Arts Building, a structure of somewhat similar architectural type to the Manufactures and Liberal Arts Building, but much more ornate externally. It is 340 feet long by 160 feet wide, and has an annex 240 by 70 feet. On the opposite side is a building, 300 feet long by 125 feet wide, of an entirely different architectural design and strongly suggestive of the old California Missions, which have, no doubt, been the source of its inspiration. This structure is the Agricultural and Horticultural Building, and contains exhibits of those products which have made California famous during the past two decades. It is undoubtedly the building whose contents will get the earliest and longest attention from the Eastern visitor, for in those contents may be said to be embodied the wonderful story of the fertility of California's soil and the rare quality of its incomparable climate. Here it is that practical expression is given, which the mind of the most incredulous must accept, to California's claim of being a land of perennial sunshine, flowing with milk and honey and oil, laden with the rich spoils of the harvest and the vintage and the blushing fruits of the orchard, and gaily adorned with the fragrant and beautiful vari-colored draperies of heath, meadow, hill and garden. Adjoining the Agricultural and Horticultural Building, on the north side, and completing the quadrangle, is the Fine Arts Building. This structure covers an area of 120 by 60 feet and is the only permanent building in the group. It will remain after the Exposition's days are ended. It is Egyptian in design, and a pair of Sphinxes occupy pedestals in front of the main entrance. It is severely plain in architectural style, but the very severity of its lines makes it one of the most attractive if not one of the most artistic buildings on the grounds. It is constructed of brick and iron. All light is secured by skylights. The ground floor has a central rotunda, the rest being divided into connecting exhibition rooms. There is a wide exhibition corridor the entire length of the building, and a gallery eighteen feet wide.

Space Awarded Foreign Exhibitors—

Foreign nations have been awarded the subjoined number of square feet in these buildings for the display of their respective exhibits:

Austro-Hungary	3,000
Belgium	500
Canada	1,000
Ceylon	2,000
France	5,000
Germany	6,000
Great Britain and East Indies	6,000
Italy	8,000
Japan	3,000
Oriental Concessions	2,000
Russia	22,000
Spain	800
Switzerland	2,000

MECHANICAL ARTS BUILDING

THE FAIR GROUNDS

Inside the Quadrangle—

Inside the quadrangle the grounds have been elaborately laid out and planted with palms and other semi-tropical plants, in evidence of the semi-tropical nature of the climate with which the northern as well as the southern part of the State is favored, and that these latitudes are virtually exempt from the dominion of King Frost.

The Electric Tower—

In the center of the quadrangle stands the electric tower, i's apex is 266 feet in the air, and an elevator carries the curious to the observation platform, an elevation of 200 feet from the ground.

Outside the Quadrangle—

Outside the group of exhibition buildings proper, constituting the quadrangle, are the various concessions made to private exhibitors and to foreign nations, and the various counties of the State.

Vienna Prater—

Adjoining the east wing of the Manufactures and Liberal Arts Building is the Vienna Prater group, comprising three main buildings and several bazaars, the concert hall being 200 by 150 feet.

Hawaiian Village and Cyclorama—

The Hawaiian Village and Cyclorama are in the same vicinity.

Santa Barbara Amphibia—

Adjoining the Cyclorama comes the Santa Barbara Amphibia, built after the style of an old Mission, and covering 76 by 56 feet.

The Chinese Pagoda—

The Chinese Pagoda stands on the opposite side of the roadway leading east toward the Middle Drive. It is 160 feet long and 90 feet wide.

The Monterey Building—

The Monterey County Building occupies a position in the rear, and represents a Mexican rancheria, the tiles on the roof having formerly been used as the covering for some of the buildings attached to the San Carlos Mission, near Carmelo Bay. It is 70 feet long by 35 feet wide.

Santa Clara County—

The Santa Clara County Building adjoins the Monterey County Building.

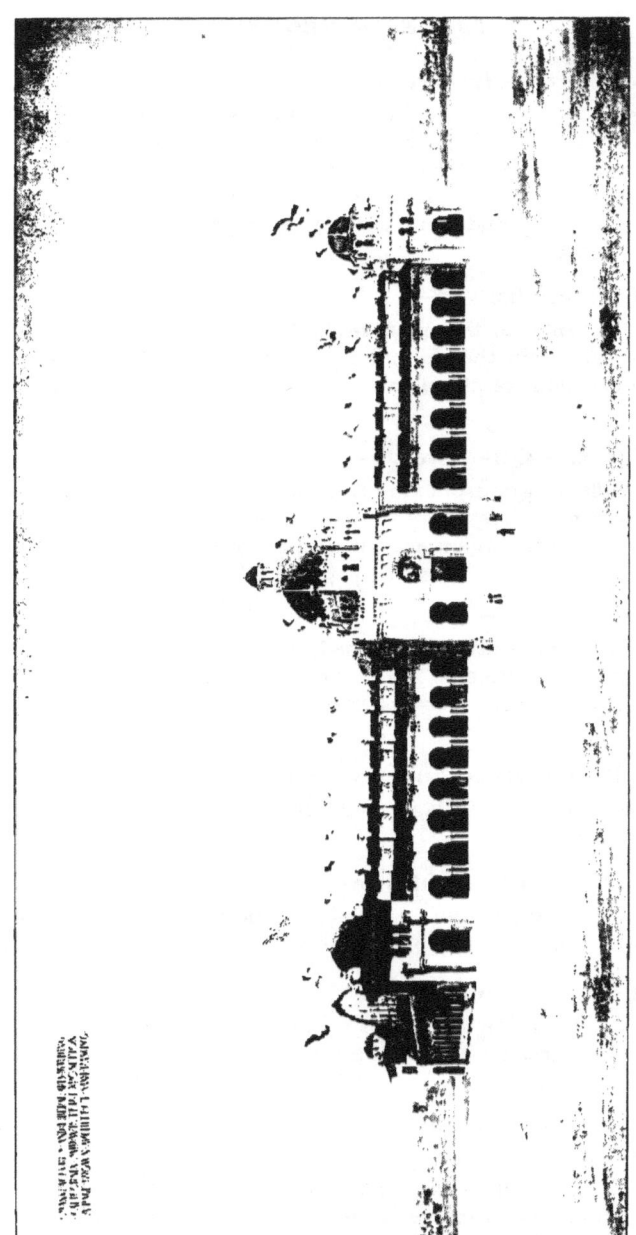

MANUFACTURES AND LIBERAL ARTS BUILDING.

The Firth Wheel—
North of the Cyclorama, and in rear of the Hawaiian Village, stands the great Firth Wheel, 225 feet in height.

Streets of Cairo—
The Oriental Concessions with the Streets of Cairo stand behind the Mechanical Arts Building and may be reached from the Middle Drive or from the road passing the north end of the last named building. It comprises three main buildings and a number of bazaars.

The German Village—
Almost at the extreme south end of the Exposition grounds is the German Village, comprising a representation of Heidelberg Castle and seven other buildings typical of German village architecture.

Japanese Village—
Four main buildings and fifteen tea houses, rockeries and fish ponds and gardens constitute the Japanese Village, situated near the northwestern corner of the quadrangle at the western end of the Agricultural Building.

Roumania, Servia and Montenegro—
The Roumanian, Servian and Montenegrin group adjoins the Japanese Village on the south.

Southern California Building—
It covers 140 feet by 125 feet. Eight counties represented, namely: Los Angeles, San Diego, Orange, Riverside, San Bernardino, Ventura, San Luis Obispo and Santa Barbara.

Northern California Building—
Contains exhibits from Sacramento, Placer, Butte, Solano, Colusa, Napa, Yuba, Siskiyou and Shasta Counties. Each county occupies in the building the space named in the following: Yuba, 950 square feet; Napa, 1400 feet; Solano, 1400 feet; Sacramento, 1400 feet; Placer, 900 feet; Butte, 900 feet; Colusa, 900 feet; Shasta, 250 feet; Siskiyou, 250 feet. This building covers 180 by 132 feet, and stands west of Administration Building.

Alameda County Building—
It covers an area 100 by 75 feet.

San Joaquin County Building—
This is a Greek cross, 140 by 100 feet, with colonnade and dome.

Mining Camp of '49—
Site 450 by 250 feet near Strawberry Hill. Includes the Nevada State Building and over twenty other structures.

Tulare County—
This county is represented by a model farm, occupying 80 by 60 feet.

Colorado Gold Mine—
Near eastern entrance to Exposition grounds.

Scenic Railway—
The Scenic Railway begins near the east gate to the Exposition grounds and follows the meanderings of the South Drive until it reaches the southern entrance to the quadrangle where it doubles on itself.

Boone's Arena—
Moorish Mirror Maze—
The Esquimaux Village—
Arizona Indian Village—
Sioux Indian Village—
Anne Hathaway's Cottage, (British)—
Are all on the south side of the South Drive.

Festival Hall—
West end of grounds. Building 141 by 133 feet; height, 72 feet.

Ostrich Farm—
One of the most interesting live exhibits on the Fair grounds is that contained in the Norwalk Ostrich Farm, which is located

on the west side of the South Drive, almost in the rear of the Administration Building. The exhibit consists of upwards of thirty ostriches, ranging in age from two months to ten years, all being from the original stock imported from South Africa in 1886. The largest bird in the collection stands eight feet high and weighs 250 pounds. Visitors to the Fair will have an opportunity of witnessing every stage in the development of an ostrich and the production of an ostrich plume. A pair of ostriches are worth from $50 to $600 according to age and quality of feathers. Every feature connected with ostrich farming in this State is quite as favorable to the industry as in South Africa, with the additional advantage that the California birds mature earlier without impairment to the value of the feathers. The exhibit is in charge of Edwin Cawston, proprietor of Norwalk Ostrich Farm, Norwalk, California, who will freely impart all information desired by visitors. The cost of admission to the exhibit is twenty-five cents.

THE FAIR GROUNDS 79

Free List at the Fair—

The admission fee to the Fair Grounds, which is paid at the entrance gate, is fifty cents. It is good for one day only, and it entitles the visitor to free access to the following buildings:

- Administration
- Agricultural and Horticultural
- Alameda County
- Anne Hathaway's Cottage (British)
- Canadian
- Central Court (including electric tower, fountains and gardens)
- Chocolate Pavilion
- Concert Stand (Iowa and Midwinter Fair Bands)
- Festival Hall
- Fine Arts
- German Tavern
- Humboldt County
- Manufactures
- Marine Café (fish on exhibition cooked to order)
- Mechanical Arts
- Monterey County
- Northern California
- Oregon
- San Joaquin County
- San Mateo County
- Santa Clara County
- Santa Cruz County
- Southern California
- Taber's Photographic
- Vienna Prater (with yodlers and round tables)
- Yaqui Pottery Makers

[Nevada State Building is enclosed in the Forty-nine Mining Camp, and is not included, therefore, in the free list.]

Side-show Charges—

After entering the Fair Grounds, there are forty-one side shows, independent of the exhibition buildings, to which the visitor gains admission by the payment of a special fee. The full list of their charges is as follows:

Admission to Fair Grounds	$0 50
Arizona Curiosities	25
Automatic Race-course	25
Balloon (captive) Grounds	10
Balloon Trip	50
Boone's Arena	50
Cairo Street	10
Camel Ride	25
Chinese Building	25
Chinese Theatre	25
Colorado Gold Mine	25
Dancing Girls	25
Dante's Inferno	25
Donkey Ride	15
Egyptian Hall	25
Electric Theatre	25
Esquimaux Village	25
Firth Wheel	25
Foote's Museum	25
Forty-nine Dance House	25

FINE ARTS BUILDING

Side-show Charges—Concluded

* Forty-nine Mining Camp	$0 25
Forty-nine Theatre	25
Grand Stand (Athletic Grounds)	25
Green's Sculpture Exhibit	25
Haunted Swing	25
Hawaiian Cyclorama	50
Hawaiian Village	25
Heidelberg Castle	10
Heidelberg Concert Hall	25
Japanese Village	25
Merry-go-round	5
Moorish Mirror Maze	25
Mummy Exhibit	10
Oriental Concert	25
Oriental Theatre	25
Oriental Village	25
Ostrich Farm	25
Phonograph	5
Roumanian Concert Hall	25
Santa Barbara Sea Lions	25
Scenic Railroad	10
White Cloud Indians	25
Total	$10 10

* The Nevada State Building is inclosed in the Forty-nine Mining Camp.

The expense, once inside the Fair Grounds, may be increased by the visitor *ad libitum* by investments in curios, mementoes, flowers and refreshments.

Cost of Fair Buildings—

The following amounts have been spent on the buildings:

Administration	$ 31,000
Agricultural and Horticultural	55,000
Annex Liberal Arts	8,500
Alameda County	5,000
Arizona Curios	4,000
Anne Hathaway's Cottage	6,000
Balloon (captive)	5,000
Boone's Arena	4,000
Canadian Headquarters	4,000
Chinese Village	15,000
Chocolate Pavilion	6,000
Dante's Inferno	3,500
Electrical Tower	80,000

Cost of Fair Buildings—Concluded

Esquimaux Village	$ 1,000
Fine Arts	55,000
Festival Hall	15,000
Flemish Dairy	1,000
Firth Wheel	35,000
Fountains (2)	30,000
Hawaiian Village	8,000
Heidelberg Schloss	10,000
Hunter's Hall	2,000
Haunted Swing	2,000
Japanese Village	4,000
Manufactures and Liberal Arts	106,000
Mechanical Arts	75,000
Mirror Maze	2,000
Mining Camp	2,500
Monterey County	5,000
Nevada State	5,000
Northern California	
Oregon	5,000
Oriental Village	45,000
Old Paris	2,000
Ostrich Farm	2,000
Roumanian	2,500
Race Course	3,000
San Joaquin County	10,000
San Mateo County	5,000
Santa Cruz County	3,000
Santa Clara County	5,000
Southern California	10,000
Santa Barbara Seals	5,000
Scenic Railroad	12,000
Yaqui Indian Village	1,000

County and State Commissioners—

Following is a list of State Commissioners:

Commissioners at Large in California—Cragie Sharp, Jr., Wm. H. Murray.
Montana—Thomas G. Merrill.
Nevada State—M. D. Foley, Evan Williams, W. E. Sharon.
Oregon State—Geo. T. Meyer and Capt. H. E. Mitchell, Portland.
Utah Territory—Secretary Chamber of Commerce, Salt Lake.
Washington State—J. T. Ronald, Seattle,

CALIFORNIA COUNTIES—

Following is a list of the California Commissioners for the various counties:

Alameda—Frank J. Moffitt, J. P. McDonald, H. W. Meek. Jas. P. Crane, C. S. Dennison, Oakland.
Alpine—Frank Smith, Markleyville.

California Counties—Continued

Amador—G. R. Breese, Chairman; J. T. Parks, Chas. L. Culbert, George Woolley.

Butte—C. L. Stilson, Chico.

Calaveras—A. L. Willie, Chairman, San Andreas; A. H. Messenger, C. M. Burleson, Otto Dolling, Capt. H. A. Messenger.

Colusa—Oscar Robinson, M. Eddy, L. F. Moulton, W. F. Ford, D. H. Arnold.

Contra Costa—A. A. Bailey, Martinez; Patrick Toomey, Hanz Rook, R. C. Leny, Chas. Montgomery, S. Fargeon, J. M. Stone, Read McCroney, E. Terry.

Del Norte—J. L. Childs, Crescent City; Judge Murphy, Frank Frantz, Thomas Duffey.

El Dorado—A. S. Basquit, Placerville.

Fresno—W. A. Shepherd, Fresno; S. W. Marshall, W. S. Badger, D. T. Fowler, F. G. Berry.

Glenn—N. K. Spect, W. A. Shoen, G. V. St. Louis.

Humboldt—Oscar D. Stem, Eureka.

Inyo—Dennis J. Hessian, Independence.

Kern—N. R. Pockard, Bakersfield.

Kings—Dr. Lucius E. Felton, Hanford; E. E. Bush, G. M. Stolp, D. Lucas.

Lake—Wm. L. Anderson, Lakeport; W. G. Young, W. A. Maxwell, Jerry Anderson, W. A. Thompson, J. Penticost, Col. C. Crawford, J. H. Cranks, F. W. Gibson, Daniel Jones, Samuel Graham, Nathan Graham, Dr. C. J. Clark.

Lassen—W. H. Burrill, Susanville.

Los Angeles—T. H. Ward, Los Angeles; J. S. Slaussen, Chairman; L. J. Rose, Charles Forman, J. W. Cook, C. D. Willard, Secretary.

Madera—J. S. Osborn, W. E. Wolf, B. W. Child, Madera.

Marin—Thos. S. Borineau, San Rafael; J. D. Sperry, George D. Shearer, George W. Burbank.

Mariposa—Maurice Newman, Mariposa.

Mendocino—Hale McGowen, Ukiah; W. D. White, W. P. Thomas, Mrs. Anna M. Reed, Carl Purdy, Chairman.

Merced—John G. Elliott, Merced; C. W. Wood, N. H. Wilson, Mrs. J. A. Robinson.

Modoc—Marion Hughes, Alturas.

Mono—J. D. Murphy, Bridgeport; J. H. Leggett, Jno. W. Kelly, R. T. Pierce, H. O. Pitts.

Monterey—T. J. Riordon, Salinas; Hon. J. D. Carr, David Jacks, Julius Trescony.

Napa—D. Shakespear, Napa; W. W. Lyman, Leonard Coates, Chas. F. Wood.

Nevada—John J. Geony, Nevada City.

Orange—D. T. Brock, Santa Ana.

Placer—John A. Fischer, Chairman, Auburn; Wm. J. May, E. W. Maslin, A. Moger, W. B. Gester, Auburn.

Plumas—W. H. Leek, Quincy.

Riverside—J. H. Newberry, Chairman, Riverside; E. E. Hamilton, F. T. Leidenberger.

Sacramento—E. Greer, Chairman, Sacramento; W. B. Hamilton, David Reese, T. B. Hall.

San Benito—G. M. Foote, Hollister; Thomas McMahon, James A. Scholefield, William Palmtag.

San Bernardino—Chas. D. Hamilton, San Bernardino; Scipio Craig, J. C. Lynch, T. S. Ingraham, Chairman.

San Diego—W. H. Holcomb, San Diego; Hanner P. McKoon, Ralph Granger, R. H. Young.

San Francisco—M. C. Haley, San Francisco.

San Joaquin—W. A. Daggett, Stockton; E. L. Conlan, E. Fisk, C. W. Yallond, M. T. Noyes, P. A. Bucil, A. Ashley, J. D. Gal, A. J. Lassen, Jos. Hoffman, Lodi.

San Luis Obispo—Chas. W. Dana, San Luis Obispo.

San Mateo—J. T. Johnson, Redwood City; C. E. Knopp, R. I. Knopp, F. P. Thompson.

CALIFORNIA COUNTIES—Concluded

Santa Barbara—P. J. Barber, Chairman, Santa Barbara; T. L. Kellogg, A. S. Cooper.
Santa Clara—S. W. Baring, San Jose; J. T. N. Burke, Philo Hersey, O. A. Hale, J. W. Ryland, T. L. Montgomery, W. E. Howley, C. N. Waster, J. H. Flickinger, W. C. Andrews, E. Goodrich, Wm. Fuller.
Santa Cruz—A. P. Stanton, Chairman, Santa Cruz; E. Martin, Henry Meyrick, S. F. Thorn, Grand Hotel, S. F.; E. G. Green, Santa Cruz.
Shasta—A. J. Deynoir, Redding; Adam Schuman, Dr. J. H. Miller, J. N. Cheaves.
Sierra—A. J. Merout, Downieville.
Siskiyou—Geo. D. Butter, Yreka; W. McBride.
Solano—R. E. Willott, Vallejo; Frank H. Bucks, F. L. Buck, Geo. A. Gillespie, E. M. McGettingan, I. Brown, R. J. Curry, D. M. Hart.
Sonoma—Wm. F. Wines, Santa Rosa; John Merritt, Jonathan Roberts, Robt. A. Poppe.
Stanislaus—J. A. Lewis, Modesto.
Sutter—B. F. Watson, Yuba City; C. R. Wilcoxon, R. C. Kells, H. B. Stabler.
Tehama—W. R. Hall, Red Bluff; R. H. Blossom, N. P. Chipman, James Copeland.
Trinity—R. L. Carter, Weaverville; E. H. Benjamin, Weaverville.
Tulare—W. H. Hammond, Visalia; G. W. Tozier, Tulare; M. J. Rouse, B. F. Bishop, Emil Newman, Philip Buyer.
Tuolumne—D. M. Ortega, Sonora; John B. Boyle.
Ventura—A. S. Kenogy, Ventura; Hon. Thomas R. Bard, N. Blackstock, F. A. Foster, E. O. Gerberding.
Yolo—R. W. Pendergast, Woodland.
Yuba—J. K. Hare, Marysville; R. W. Skinner, E. A. Forbes, W. B. Meek, J. H. Durst, J. R. Trainor, W. T. Ellis, Jr., G. W. Hainey, Louis Conrath, Jas. O. Gates.

Foreign Commissioners—

Following are the names of the Foreign Commissioners:

Argentine Republic—Don Carlos Gallardo, Commissioner-General.
Austria-Hungary—Raphael Kuhe, Commissioner-General; O. Moser, Assistant Commissioner.
Belgium—Emile Ramlot, Commissioner-General.
Dominion of Canada—A. C. Oldenburg, Commissioner-General.
Denmark—Vice-Consul Otto A. Dreier, Commissioner-General.
France—Leopold Bonet, Commissioner-General; F. W. Hemler and Hugo Benedix, Assistants Commissioner-General.
German Empire—Herman Hillger, Commissioner-General.
Great Britain and British Colonies—J. H. Stiles, Commissioner-General.
Republic of Honduras—Dr. W. T. Thackeray, Commissioner-General.
Italy—Chevalier T. Solombra, Commissioner-General; A. Mackie, Assistant Commissioner-General and Commissioner of Manufactures.
Japan—Frans A. Koidzumi, Commissioner-General; V. J. Zola, Assistant Commissioner-General.
Republic of Liberia—Consul William Edmundorf Rothery, Commissioner-General.
Republic of Mexico—Colonel George M. Green, Commissioner-General.
Monaco—A. Mackie, Commissioner-General.
Netherlands—E. Wilkins, Commissioner-General.
Oriental Countries—Count E. de Valcourt Vermont, Commissioner-General; Albert Souhami, Assistant Commissioner-General.
Portugal—Alexandre Michelson, Commissioner-General.
Roumania, Servia and Montenegro—Consul W. E. von Johannson, Commissioner-General.
Russia—Gregoire Gelesnogradoff, Commissioner-General.
Spain—Frederick Mayer, Commissioner-General.
Norway—Maurice Lundin, Commissioner-General.
Swiss Republic—Benno Obermayer, Commissioner-General.
Republic of Costa Rica—Theodore H. Mangel, Commissioner-General.
Republic of Guatemala—Charles W. Kohlsaat, Commissioner-General.
Ceylon—J. R. Foster, Commissioner-General.

Days Set for Special Celebrations—

The following dates have been set for special celebrations:
January 1st—Opening Day.
January 27th—Dedication Day.
January 29th—Butte County Day.
February 8th—Musical Festival; Pacific Coast Bill Posters' Association.
February 9th—Pacific Association of Fire Chiefs.
February 10th—Amateur Athletic Association Sports.
February 12th—Independent Order of Good Templars.
February 14th—North Dakota.
February 15th—State of Idaho.
February 17th—Elks' Day; Amateur Athletic Association Sports.
February 19th—Southern California.
February 20th—Young Men's Institute.
February 21st—Santa Cruz County.
February 22d—N. G. C. Tournament; California Bankers.
February 23d—State of Maryland; Commercial High School and California Bankers' Association; Children's Day.
February 24th—Amateur Athletic Association Sports.
February 27th—San Bernardino County.
February 28th—French Colony.
March 3d—Amateur Athletic Association Sports.
March 8th—Vermont Day.
March 9th—University of Pacific; Japanese Day.
March 10th—Russian Day.
March 12th—State of Michigan.
March 13th—Teachers' Congress.
March 14th—Sierra County; Italian Reception.
March 15th—Maine Day.
March 16th—Geographical Congress.
March 17th—St. Patrick's Day; Irish Sports.
March 19th—San Francisco's Day; Mystic Argonauts.
March 20th—Musicians' Union.
March 22d—State of Nevada and Ventura County.
March 23d—Stanford University.
March 24th—Amateur Athletic Association Sports.
March 26th—Oregon Day.
March 28th—Santa Barbara Day.
March 29th—Kern County Day.
March 31st—Amateur Athletic Association Sports.
April 2d—Canadian Day.
April 3d—Knights and Ladies of Honor.
April 4th—Press Congress.
April 5th—State of Indiana.
April 6th—Girls' High School; Kansas Day.
April 9th—Belgian Day.
April 10th—San Diego.

Days Set for Special Celebrations—Continued

April 11th—University of California.
April 12th—Order of Chosen Friends.
April 13th—Fresno County.
April 14th—Amateur Athletic Association Sports.
April 16th—Oakland High School; Catholic Ladies' Aid Society.
April 17th—Ancient Order of Foresters; Companions of the Forest.
April 18th—Grocers' Day.
April 19th—Humboldt County.
April 20th—Native Sons and Daughters of the Golden West.
April 21st—Amateur Athletic Association Sports.
April 23d—Poet's Day, Shakespeare's Day; St. George's Society.
April 24th—Austrian Empire; Horticultural Congress.
April 25th—I. O. O. F. and California Volunteers.
April 26th—I. O. O. F. and Daughters of Rebekah.
April 27th—Grand Army of the Republic.
April 28th—Boys' Brigade.
April 30th—Danish Day.
May 1st—California Day; Our Children's Day.
May 2d—Colored Americans.
May 3d—Merced and Mariposa; College Professors' Ass'n.
May 4th—Firemen's Day; South Dakota Day.
May 5th—Steam Engineers; Olympic Club.
May 7th—San Rafael Rose Festival; Cal. Pharmacy Society.
May 8th—Mendocino County; College of Pharmacy.
May 9th—German Day, Mayday Festival.
May 10th—Solano County; University Debates.
May 11th—Mills Seminary; Viticultural Day.
May 12th—Independent Order of Red Men; Tammany.
May 14th—Swedish Day.
May 15th—Old Friends.
May 16th—United Ancient Order of Druids.
May 17th—State of Minnesota; Norwegian Day.
May 18th—Women's Christian Temperance Union; San Mateo.
May 19th—Knights of Pythias.
May 21st—Medical Congress; St. Mary's College.
May 22d—Miners' Congress.
May 23d—Butchers' Day.
May 24th—British Empire Day.
May 25th—Napa County.
May 26th—Letter Carriers' Day.
May 28th—Eastern California Pioneers.
May 29th—Kings County Day; Hahnemann College.
May 30th—Decoration Day; Memorial Services and Parade.

Days Set for Special Celebrations—Concluded

May 31st—Oriental, or Ottoman, Day.
June 1st—Aldermen's Day.
June 2d—Italian Day; Foreign Military Tournament.
June 4th—Monterey County.
June 5th—North and South Carolina.
June 6th—St. Ignatius and Santa Clara Colleges; Maine Day.
June 7th—Portuguese Day and "The Berlins."
June 8th—Horticultural Day.
June 9th—Ancient Order of Foresters of America.
June 11th—Hawaiian Day.
June 12th—Texas Day; California Medical College.
June 13th—Dental Association.
June 14th—Santa Clara County.
June 15th—Swiss Day; Sonoma County.
June 16th—Scotch Day and Scottish Sports.
June 18th—Bunker Hill and Tuolumne County Reunion.
June 19th—Ancient Order of United Workmen.
June 20th—Sacramento Day.
June 21st—San Francisco Federation of Women.
June 22d—Montenegro, Servia and Roumania Day.
June 23d—Finlandish Day.
June 25th—Tulare County.
June 26th—Woodmen of the World.
June 27th—Cooper Medical College.
June 28th—Pacific Coast Commercial Travelers.
June 29th—Spanish Day.
June 30th—Sunset Day.

NOTE—

On every Saturday, whether noted or not in the foregoing list, Amateur Athletic Association Sports will be included in the programme.

Sunday at the Fair—

The Midwinter Exposition will be open every day through the season, Sundays included; but no special arrangement has been made by the Executive Committee for the latter in the list of "Special Days." Sunday dates have, consequently, been omitted from the foregoing list.

Foreign Consuls—

Foreigners visiting the Fair desiring to confer with the local representatives of their respective nations will find the following list of service:

Argentine Republic—J. L. Schleiden, Consul, 207 Battery.
Austro-Hungarian Empire—Francis Korbel, Consul, 308 Battery.
Belgium—Wilfrid B. Chapman, Consul, C. L. Tamm, Vice-Consul, 123 California.

Foreign Consuls—Concluded

Bolivia—F. Herrera, Consul, 218 California.

Brazil—D. L. Randolph, Vice-Consul, 12 Montgomery.

Chile—Nephtali Guerrero, Consul-General, 621 Clay; W. D. Catton, Vice-Consul, 430 California.

China—Li Yung Yew, Consul-General; King Owyang, Vice-Consul, 806 Stockton.

Columbia—Adolfo Canal, Consular Agent, 319 California.

Costa Rica—Rafael Gallegos, Consul-General, 230 California.

Denmark—J. Simpson, Consul, 22 California.

Ecuador—John T. Wright, Consul, 640 Market.

France—L. de Lalande, Consul; E. A. Pesoli, Vice-Consul, 604 Commercial.

German Empire—Adolph Rosenthal, Consul-General; Oswald Lohan, Vice-Consul, 318 Sacramento.

Great Britain—Denis Donohoe, Consul; Wellesley Moore, Vice-Consul, 506 Battery.

Greece—D. G. Camarinos, Consul, 519 Sansome.

Guatemala—J. Diaz Duran, Consul, 204 Front, room 18.

Hawaiian Islands—Charles S. Wilder, Consul-General, 206 Sansome.

Honduras—John T. Wright, Consul, 640 Market.

Italy—G. Branchi, Consul-General; Cesare Poma, Vice-Consul, 506 Battery.

Japan—Sutemi Chinda, Consul, Phelan Building.

Mexico—Alex. K. Coney, Consul-General, 604 Clay.

Netherlands—James de Fremery, Consul; W. C. B. de Fremery, Vice-Consul, 530 California.

Nicaragua—William L. Merry, Consul-General, 204 Front, room 2.

Paraguay—P. J. Van Loben Sells, Consul.

Peru—J. Emilio Lassus, Consul-General, 606 Montgomery.

Portugal—J. de Costa Duarte, Consul, 605 Clay; H. Laidley, Vice-Consul, 323 Montgomery.

Russia—Vladimir Arisimovitch, Consul; Horace G. Platt, Vice-Consul, 411¼ California.

Roumania—W. E. Von Johannsen, Consul, 220 California.

Salvador—J. M. Roma, Consul, 123 California.

Spain—Jorge Madrilley, Consul, 411½ California.

Sweden and Norway—Henry Lund, 214 California.

Switzerland—Antoine Borel, Consul, 311 Montgomery.

Turkey—George E. Hall, Consul, 329 Market.

Uruguay—Jose Costa, Consul, 330 Montgomery.

Venezuela—Alexander E. Grogan, Consul, 318 California.

Spanish Nomenclature.

✱ ✱ ✱

Names of Places and Things

From Indian and Spanish Sources.

✱ ✱ ✱

Many names which the tourist will hear mentioned in California are of Spanish or Indian derivation, and will consequently sound unfamiliar. The following is a list of the majority of the names in common use, with their meaning and, what is of much more value to the uninitiated, their pronunciation.

ADONDE (ah-*don*-day). Where to.
AGUA CALIENTE (*ah*-gua cal-e-*ain*-tay). Hot water.
ALAMEDA (ah-lah-*may*-dah). Lit., a grove of poplars; a shaded walk.
ALAMILLO (ah-lah-*meel*-yo). A place of poplars.
ALBUQUERQUE (*al*-boo-ker-kay). A family name.
ALCATRAZ (*al*-cat-*ras*). Pelican.
ALGODONES (al-go *do*-nais). Lit., cottons; cotton lands.
ALISO (all-*ee*-so) Alder-bush.
ALMADEN (al-mah-*dain*). A place of mineral deposits.
ALTURAS (al *too*-ras). Heights.
ALVARADO (alvar-*ah*-da). A launching place for ships.
ALVISO (al-*ve*-so). A view.
AMADOR (ah-mah-*dor*). Lover.
ARROYO, OR ARROYO SECO (ar-*ro*-yo *say*-co). A wash made by water; not a creek or river, and shallower than a canyon.
AZUSA (ah-*soo*-sah). A provocation; annoyance. The word is colloquial.
BALLONA (bal-*yo*-nah). If spelled Ballina (bal-*ye*-nah), it would mean whale.
BELLA VISTA (*bail*-ya *vees*-tah). Pretty view.
BENICIA (ben-*ee*-shah). Should be Venecia; Venice.
BERNAL (ber-*nal*). Proper name.
BERNALILLO (ber-nal-*ee*-yo). Little Bernal.
BUENAVENTURA (b'*wain*-ah-vain-*too*-rah). Good fortune; also, a frequent proper name.
BUENA VISTA (b'*wain*-ah *vees*-tah). Good view.
CAJON (cah *hone*) Caja, a box; cajon, a big box; Cajon Pass, "box pass."
CALAVERAS (cal ah-*vay*-ras). Plu. Rattle-pates; mad-caps; didoes.
CANYON DIABLO, CANYON. The Spanish spelling is "cañon," and pronounced can-on by persons not accustomed. The Spanish pronunciation is can-*yone*; the American, can-yon. It means the bore of a gun: calibre; a groove; in artillery, the gun itself. As used ordinarily it means a ravine with steep sides between hills or mountains, or a deep fissure. CANYON DIABLO (de-*ah* blo), Devil's canyon; canyoncito (*see*-to), little canyon.
CARMELITA (carmel-*e*-tah). A flower.
CASA GRANDE (*cah* sah *gran*-day). Big house.
CARRIZO (carr-*ee* so). A reed grass.
CERRO GORDO (sair-ro *gor*-do). Thick ridge.
CERILLOS, LOS (sair eel-*yose*. Plu. Small round hills.
CERITOS (sair-*e*-tose). Little ridges.
CHAVES (*chah*-vais). A family name.
CHICO (*che*-co). Little.
CHINO (*che*-no). A Chinaman.
CIENEGA (se-*ain*-e-ga). A swamp.
COLORADO (co-lo-*rah*-do). Red.
CORDERO (cor-*day*-ro). A lamb.
CORONADO (co-ro-*nah*-do). A family name. Lit., "The Crowned."
CORRAL (cor-*ral*). A pen; an outdoor inclosure.

CUCAMONGA (ku-cah-*mon*-ga). If this word were spelled with a "j" in the place of the "g," the word would mean an uncomplimentary reflection on a nun.
DE LUZ (day *loos*). Lit., of light.
DEL MAR (dail-*mar*). Of the sea.
DOS CABEZAS (dose cah-*bay*-sas). Two heads.
DOS PALMAS (dose *pahl*-mas. Two palms.
DOS VALLES (dose *val*-yais). Two valleys.
EL DORADO (ail do-*rah*-do). The golden; in modern use "dorado" means gilt, washed.
EL MOLINO (ail mo-*lee*-no). The mill.

EL MONTE (ail *mon*-tay). The wood.
EL PASO (ail *pah*-so). The pass.—DEL NORTE (dail *nor*-te). The pass of the North.
EL RITO (ail *ree*-to). The rite; the ceremony.
ENCINITAS (ain-say-*ne*-tas). Little oaks.
ESPERANZA (ais-per-*an*-sa). Hope.
ESTRELLA (ais-*trail*-yah). A star.
FARRALLONES (fair-al-*yo*-nais). Plu. Small peaked islands rising out of the sea. FAROL (fah-*role*). A beacon.
FRESNO (*frais*-no). Ash tree.
GALLINAS (gal-*ye*-nas). Hens.

GARCIA (gar-*ce*-ah). A family name; equivalent of Smith or Jones.
GARROTE (gar-*ro*-tay). Instrument for capital punishment.
GAVANZO (gar-*van*-so). A pea; pea vine or bloom.
GAVILAN (gah-ve-*lan*). A hawk.
GAVIOTA (gah-ve-o-tah). A sea-gull.
GOLETA (go-*lay*-tah). A schooner.
GRACIOSA (gran-se-*oh*-sah). Kind.
GRANADA (gran-*ah*-dah). A pomegranate; renowned; powerful; fruitful.
HERMOSILLO (air-mo-*seel*-yo). Little beauty. HERMOSA (air-*mo*-sah). Beautiful.
HORNITOS (or-*ne*-tose.) Little ovens. HORNO (*or*-no), an oven.
HUALAPAI (*whal*-a-pah-e).
INDIO (*een*-de-o). Indian.
JICARILLO (hic-ah-*reel*-yo). Should be spelled Jacarillo. A braggart, a boaster.
JIMENEZ (he-*may*-nais). A family name.
JORNADA (hor-*nah*-dah). A journey. JORNADA DEL MUERTO (dail M'*uer*-to), the journey of death.
LAS ANIMAS (lahs *ah*-ne-mas). Plu. The souls.
LA CAÑADA (lah can-*yah*-dah). The glen; a vale.
LAS CASITAS (lahs cah *se*-tas). Plu. The little houses.
LAS CRUCES (lahs *croo*-sais). The crosses.
LAGUNA (lah-*goo*-nah). A lake.
LA JOYA (la *ho*-yah). The jewel.
LA PANZA (lah *pan*-sah). The paunch.
LA PUENTA (lah-*p'wain*-tay). The point of land.
LA PUNTA (lah *poon*-tah). The point.
LAS FLORES (lahs *flo*-rais). The flowers.
LA JUNTA (lah *hoon*-tah). The junction.
LAS VEGAS (lahs *vay*-gas). The meadows.
LERDO (*lehr*-do). Dull; obtuse; thick-headed.
LINDA (*leen*-dah). Pretty.
LOBOS (*lo*-bose). Plu. Wolves.
LOS ALAMOS (lose *ahl*-ah-mose). Plu. The poplars.
LOS ANGELES (los *on*-hel-ais). Plu. The angels.
LOS CUEROS (lose *quer*-ose). Plu. The hides.
LOS GATOS (lose *gah*-tose). Plu. The cats.
LOS LOMOS (lose *lo*-mose). Plu. The hills.
LOS MEDANOS (lose may-*dan*-os). Plu. Sandbanks on the sea-shore.
LOS NIETOS (lose nee *a*-tos). Plu. The grandchildren.
LOS ROBLES (lose *ro*-blais). Plu. The oaks.
MADERA (mah-*day*-rah). Wood in general.
MADRON, madrono (mah-*drone*). Name of tree.
MANITOU (*man* ay-to). The Supreme Power.
MANUELITO (man-wale-e-to). Little Emanuel.
MANZANITO (man-zahn-e-to). Lit. Little apple. A California shrub.
MARIPOSA (mah-re-*po*-sah). Butterfly.
MENDOCINO (men-do-*se* no). Lit. A little liar.
MERCED (mer-*said*). Mercy.
MESA (may-sah). Table land.
MESILLA (may-*seel*-yah). Little flat-topped hill.
MESQUITE (mes-*keet*). A shrub of the acacia family.
MILPITAS (meel-*pec*-tas). Lit. A thousand whistles.
MODESTO (mo-*dais*-to). Modest.
MONTE DIABLO (*mon*-tay dee-*ah*-blo). Devil mountain.
MONTECITO (*mon*-tay-*se*-to). Little mountain.
MONTEREY (mon-tay-*ray*). King's mountain.
MORENA (mo-*ray*-na). Brown.
NACIMIENTO (nah-se-me-*ain*-to). Lit. A birth.
NOGALES (no-*gal*-ais). Plu. Walnut trees.
OLLITA (ole-*ye*-tah). A little water jar. Sometimes spelled on maps "Oleta."
ORO GRANDE (*gran*-day). Lit. Big gold.
PACHECO (pah-*chay*-co). A harmless little fellow.
PAJARO (*pah*-hah-ro). A bird.
PALA (*pah*-lah). A wooden shovel.
PASADENA (pas-ah-*day*-nah). Probably a corruption of "Pah-so-deh-*dain*," "Gate of Eden."
PASO ROBLES (*pah*-so *ro*-blais). Oak pass.
PESCADERO (pais-cah-*day*-ro). A fishing place.
PICACHO (pe-*cah*-cho). Peak.
PINOLE (pe-*no*-lay). Parched corn, ground and mixed with sugar and water as a drink, or used as food.
PIÑON (peen-*yone*). A nut-bearing pine.
PLACER (play-*sair*). The place near a stream where free gold is found. Pleasure.
PLUMAS (*ploo*-mas). Feathers.
PONCHO (pone-*cho*). A cloak like a square or round blanket with a slit in the center for the head to pass through.
POTRERO (po-*tray*-ro). A place for raising colts; stock-farm.

PRESIDIO (pray-*see*-de-o). A garrison of soldiers; a penitentiary.
PUENTE (p'*wain*-tay). A point of land.
RANCHO, RANCHITA, etc. Farm buildings.
RATON (rah-*tone*). A mouse. Rata (*rah*-tah) means a rat.
RIO, RIO VISTA, RIO GRANDE, etc. (*re*-oh *vees*-tay; *gran*-day). A river, river view, big river.
ROSARIO (ro-*sah* re-o). A rosary.
SACRAMENTO (sah-crah-*main*-to). A sacrament.
SALINAS (sal-*e*-nas). Places of salt.
SAN ANDREAS (and-*rais*). Saint Andrews.
SAN ANTONIO (an-*tone*-yo). St. Anthony.
SAN BERNARDINO (ber-nard-*e*-no). St. Bernard.
SAN DIMAS (de-*mas*). St. Demas.
SAN DIEGO (de-*a*-go). St. James.
SAN DIEGUITO (de-a-*ge* to). Little St. James.
SAN FERNANDO. St. Ferdinand.
SAN GABRIEL (gab-re-*ail*). St. Gabriel.
SAN GORGONIO (gor-*gone*-yo). St. Gregory.
SAN JACINTO (hah-*seen*-to). St. Jacinth.
SAN JOSÉ (ho-*say*). St. Joseph.
SAN JUAN (h'*wan*). St. John.
SAN JUAN CAPISTRANO (cah-pees-*tran*-o). St. John the chanter.
SAN JOAQUIN (h'wah-*keen*). St. Joaquin.
SAN MARCIAL (mar-ce-*al*). St. Martial.
SAN MATEO (mat-*a*-o). St. Matthew.
SAN MIGUEL (me-*gail*). St. Michael.
SAN PABLO (*pah*-blo). St. Paul.
SAN PASCUAL (pahs-*qual*). Holy Easter.
SAN PEDRO (*pay*-dro). St. Peter.
SAN RAFAEL (rah-*fah*-ail). St. Raphael.
SAN TOMAS. St. Thomas.
SANTA ANA; ANITA (*ah*-nah; an-*ne*-tah). St. Ann; little St. Ann; pronounced Santa*nah*, Santa*ne*tah.
SANTA BARBARA. St. Barbara.
SANTA CATALINA (cat-ah-*le*-nah). St. Catherine.
SANTA CLARA. St. Clara.
SANTA CRUZ (croos). Holy Cross.
SANTA FE (*fay*). Holy Faith.
SANTA MONICA (*mon*-e-cah). St. Monica.
SAPINERO (sah-pe-*nay*-ro). Sapino, a kind of pine; a grove of such.
SAUSALITO (sow-sah-*le*-to). A little willow.
SEPULVIDA (say-*pool*-ve-dah.)
SIERRA MADRE (se-*ata* rah *mad*-ray). Mother Range.
SOBRANTE (so-*bran*-tay). Rich; wealthy; surplus; overflow.
SOCORRO (só-*co*-ro). Succor; relief.
SOLEDAD (so-lay-*dad*). Solitude; lonesomeness.
SOLANA (so-*lah*-na). Sunny place; sunshine.
TAMALPAIS (tam-ahl-*pah*-ees). The country of tamales.
TEMECULA (tay-*mec*-oo-lah).
TIBURON (tee-boo-*rone*). A shark.
TIAJUANA (te-a *wha* na). One word. TIA JUANA; Aunt Jane.
TIMPAS (*leem*-pahs).
TRINIDAD (tre-ne-*dad*). The Trinity.
TULARE (tu-*lar*-a). A place of rushes.
VACAVILLE (*vah*-cah). Vaca, a cow, Cowville.
VALLEJO (val-*lay*-ho). A little valley.
VARA (*var*-ah). Spanish yard measure; a wand, a switch.
YOSEMITE (yo-*sem*-e-tay). Said to mean a large grizzly bear.
YSIDORA (ee-se-*do*-rah). Isadore; a woman's name.

Itineraries for Tourists.

★ ★ ★

Pleasant Trips to Pleasant Places for Pleasure Seekers.

★ ★ ★

The following itineraries, which we are able to print through the courtesy of *The Traveler*, of San Francisco, will be of interest to the visitor to the Fair who desires to see and enjoy something outside of San Francisco. To avoid the possibility of misleading the reader, it is proper to state here, however, that the time schedule of the railroads, connecting with the various places named, is liable to change any day. To insure certainty, therefore, the tourist contemplating visiting either of the places named ought to consult the latest railroad time card. The main value of the time card, here inserted, is to show how much time is really covered in either of these itineraries.

A SLEIGH-RIDE AND A SKATE IN CALIFORNIA

Leave San Francisco .... 5:00 P. M. Saturday
Arrive Truckee ....5:55 A. M. Sunday

Breakfast at the Truckee Hotel at the depot. At Franzini Bros. stable you can secure a two-horse sleigh, and after a ride of two and a half miles arrive at Donner Lake about 8:00 A. M. Take your lunch with you. Here you can skate all day and have a good time generally. Returning, leave Donner Lake about dusk, enjoy a moonlight drive over the snow, dine at Truckee, and take the train at midnight, reaching San Francisco at 10:45 A. M. Monday.

Railroad fare (round trip) $15 60
Pullman berth   "   " 3 00
Sleigh for four "   " .... each person 1 00

NAPA SODA SPRINGS

Leave San Francisco .... 4:00 P. M. Saturday
Arrive Napa .... 6:25 P. M. Saturday
Arrive Napa Soda Springs .... 7:25 P. M. Saturday
Leave Napa Soda Springs .... 6:30 A. M. Monday
Arrive San Francisco .... 9:45 A. M. Monday

The stage ride from Napa to the Springs (seven miles) is one of the most picturesque in the State. The Springs are 1,000 feet above the level of the valley. Sunday can be most pleasantly spent there, the natural mineral water direct from the bubbling spring being free to guests.

Railroad fare (round trip) $2 00
Stage fare   "   " 1 00

PASO ROBLES SPRINGS

Leave San Francisco .... 8:15 A. M. Saturday
Arrive Paso Robles Springs .... 4:19 P. M. Saturday
Leave Paso Robles Springs .... 10:13 A. M. Monday
Arrive San Francisco .... 6:10 P. M. Monday

There is no pleasanter day's ride out of San Francisco than this. The ocean is twice sighted, and a glimpse of two of California's proudest institutions. viz.: Leland Stanford, Junior, University and the Lick Observatory, are to be had en route.

Railroad fare (round trip)............................. .... $12 40

DEL MONTE, SANTA CRUZ AND SAN JOSE

Leave San Francisco ....2:30 P. M. Saturday
Arrive Hotel del Monte ....6:15 P. M. Saturday
Leave   "   "   ....1:38 P. M. Sunday
Arrive Santa Cruz (Sea Beach Hotel) ....3:40 P. M. Sunday
Leave   "   "   ....2:00 P. M. Monday

SOUTH OF SAN FRANCISCO TO MONTEREY

Arrive San Jose (Hotel Vendome) ....4:10 P. M. Monday
Leave   "   "   ....9:00 A. M. Tuesday
Arrive San Francisco ....10:50 A. M. Tuesday

From San Francisco to Del Monte and Del Monte to Santa Cruz you take the broad-gauge route; from Santa Cruz to San Francisco, the narrow-gauge route through the Santa Cruz Mountains. At Del Monte you will have ample time to see the beautiful grounds and take the famous eighteen-mile drive. At the Sea Beach Hotel, Santa Cruz, you are constantly in view of the ocean and the bathing grounds. From here a beautiful ride may be taken to the Big Trees, only seven miles distant. From the Hotel Vendome, San Jose, you can take interesting drives to the New Almaden Mines, twelve miles, Santa Clara, three-and-a-half miles, or Alum Rock Springs, seven miles. A stay of one day longer at San Jose will give you an opportunity to make the trip to the Lick Observatory at Mount Hamilton, twenty-seven miles from San Jose, leaving the latter point at 7:30 A. M., and returning to San Jose about 6:00 P. M. Round-trip rate from San Jose, $4.00.

Round-trip railroad ticket from San Francisco, good for six months, and including the above itinerary, $7.30.

PARAISO SPRINGS

Leave San Francisco............................ 8:15 A. M. Saturday
Arrive Soledad................................. 1:43 P. M. Saturday
Arrive Paraiso .... 2:45 P. M. Saturday
Leave   "   ....11:45 A. M. Monday
Arrive San Francisco........................... 6:10 P. M. Monday

Paraiso has an altitude of 1,400 feet above the sea-level, and is both a summer and winter resort. Here you can enjoy a delightful plunge bath, and partake of the iron, soda or sulphur springs. The beauty of its surroundings, and the character of its several springs, have justly earned for Paraiso the title of "Carlsbad of America."

Round-trip fare to the Springs.................................$9 00

BYRON HOT SPRINGS

Leave San Francisco............................9:00 A. M. Saturday
Arrive Byron Springs..........................12:15 P. M. Saturday
Leave Byron Springs........................... 9:00 A. M. Monday
Arrive San Francisco..........................12:15 P. M. Monday

This trip is most pleasant, and includes a short carriage drive of two miles from Byron Station to the Springs without charge. Byron Springs is essentially a place of rest and recuperation, and is famous for the remarkable curative properties of its waters and baths.

Fare, one way..$1 90
Round trip, Friday to Monday...................................$3 00

THE GEYSERS

Leave San Francisco (S. F. & N. P. Ry.).........7:40 A. M. Saturday
Arrive Cloverdale..............................11:30 A. M. Saturday
Arrive Geysers................................. 3:30 P. M. Saturday
Leave Geysers.................................. 9:00 A. M. Monday
Arrive Cloverdale.............................. 2:00 P. M. Monday
Arrive San Francisco........................... 6:10 P. M. Monday

Round-trip tickets (unlimited), $8.50. This includes stage, sixteen miles. Both the baths and guide through Geyser Canon are free to guests. Round-trip rail and stage ticket, including one week's board at the Geysers, $23.50.

The Geysers may be also reached via Calistoga, from which point the stage ride is twenty-six miles, and the arriving time two hours later. Fare is the same. Round-trip ticket, going by one route and returning by another, $11.50.

YOSEMITE VALLEY

Leave San Francisco............................4:00 P. M. Saturday
Arrive Raymond ....5:50 A. M. Sunday
Leave   "   (Stage)........................6:30 A. M. Sunday
Arrive Wawona..................................6:00 P. M. Sunday
Leave   "   ....7:00 A. M. Monday
Arrive Yosemite................................ Noon Monday
Leave   "   ....6:00 A. M. Tuesday
Arrive San Francisco...........................9:45 A. M. Thursday

Pullman Sleeper between San Francisco and Raymond, $1.50 per berth. The above itinerary and rate includes side trip to the Calaveras Big Trees.

San Francisco to Yosemite and return.........................$50.00

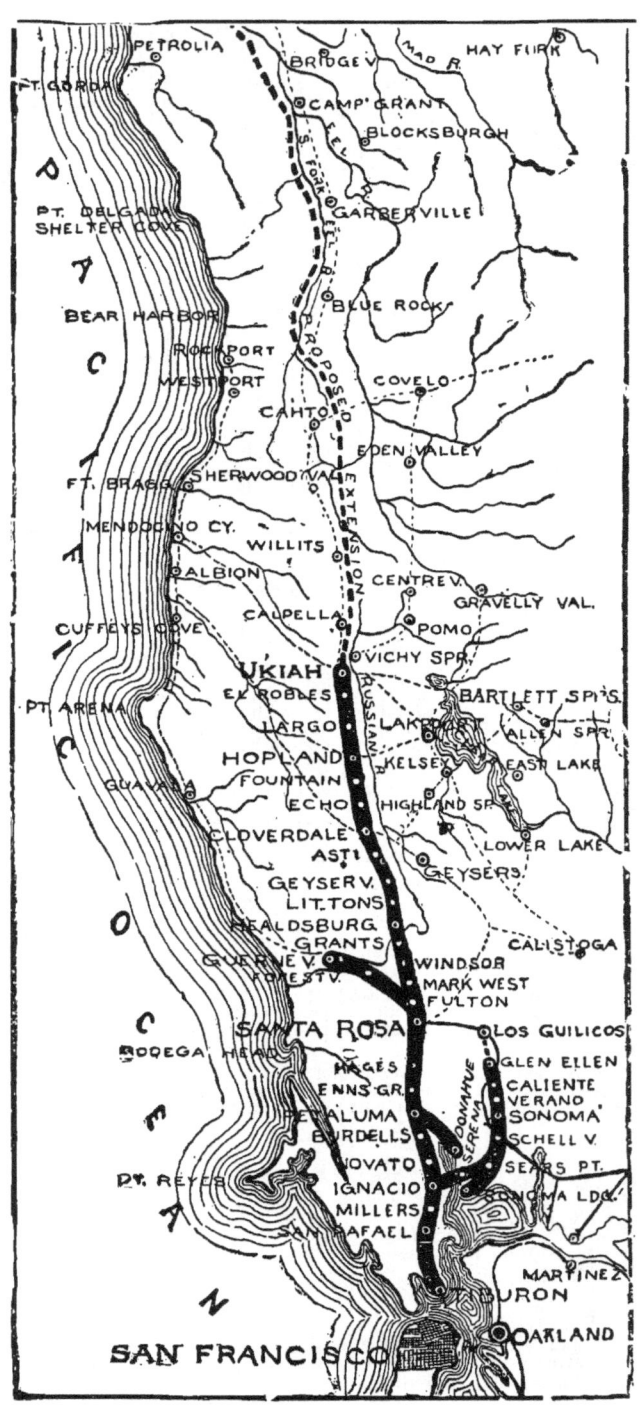

NORTH OF SAN FRANCISCO TO UKIAH
(San Francisco and North Pacific Railroad Route)

CAZADERO

Leave San Francisco	1:45 P. M. Saturday
Arrive Cazadero	7:00 P. M Saturday
Leave "	5:00 A. M. Monday
Arrive San Francisco	10:25 A. M. Monday

At Cazadero you can enjoy a hunt, fish, swim or ride through the Redwoods. The ride by rail on the North Pacific Coast is one of the most picturesque in California.

Round trip from San Francisco..................................$5.00

PICTURESQUE RUSSIAN RIVER VALLEY

The resident of San Francisco, to enjoy good health, requires an occasional outing. The winds and fogs of this city are chilling. No matter where a person lives, a change is desirable, and the citizens of this State have a boom in our glorious and varied climate. A few hours' ride in any part of the State affords relief, but no portion possesses this advantage to so great an extent as San Francisco. Within one hour's ride our people can experience a complete change of climate on the San Francisco & North Pacific Railway. At a distance of fifteen miles you reach San Rafael, with its delightful climate and beautiful residences. There is no more inviting spot in California. It is about five hours' ride through the Marin, Sonoma and Sanel valleys to the terminus of the road at Ukiah. Beautiful towns like Petaluma, Santa Rosa and Healdsburg greet the eye, whilst the country *en route*, under a high state of cultivation, blooms like a garden. On either side rise the foothills, and beyond, the mountains. Branches take you to Sonoma and Glen Ellen and Sebastopol, nestling in the Sonoma and Russian River valleys, and Guerneville, the home of the redwoods. For picturesqueness the ride along the Russian River, from Cloverdale to Ukiah, cannot be excelled. At our very doors we have all that is beautiful in nature and lovely in climate. The management of the road is liberal, and affords an opportunity to all, rich and poor, to seek that change so desirable. Three-day excursions tickets are sold at greatly reduced rates, and on Sunday half rates govern to all points. If you have time, take a rod or a gun for the finest fishing and hunting in the State. A hundred streams alive with trout and other fish are tributary to the San Francisco & North Pacific Railway.

A postal to Mr. J. P. Kirkpatrick, Manager Palace Hotel, San Francisco, will bring you, without charge, a new and elaborate souvenir. An ivory cover, with parchment and plate paper within, beautifully illustrated, forms an elgant album that is well worth the asking.

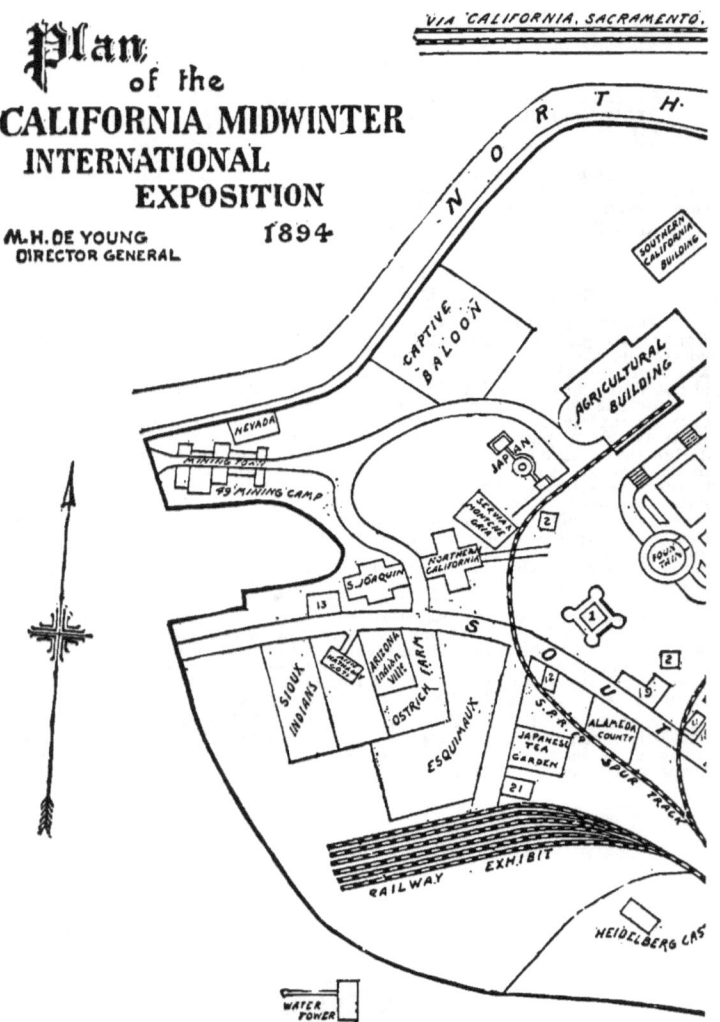

NOTE—Buildings whose space did not allow writing a distinct name are marked with figures, and appear below.

1.—Administration Building.
2.—Restaurants.
3.—Chocolate Restaurants.
4.—Firth Wheel.
5.—Santa Barbara Amphibia.
6.—Mirror Maze.
7.—Riding Gallery.
8.—Colorado Gold Mine.

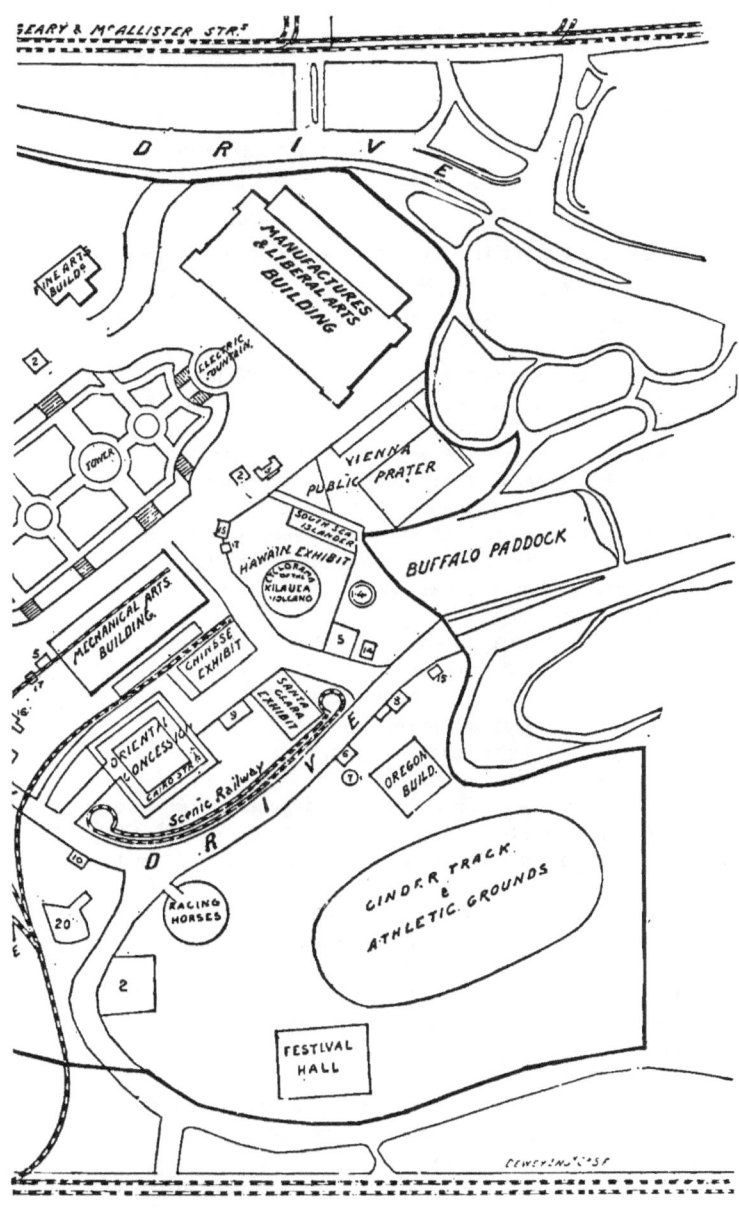

9.—Monterey Exhibit.
10.—Moorish Exhibit.
11.—Tomale Village.
12.—Arizona Museum.
13.—Canada.
14.—Dante's Inferno.
15.—Waffle Houses.
16.—Taber's Photograph Stand.
17.—Oyster Cocktail House.
18.—Haunted Swing.
19.—Aquarium.
20.—Boone's Wild Animals.
21.—Old Paris.

Amusements—Places of

★ ★ ★

San Francisco

★ ★ ★

Performances at the Theaters commence 8 P. M. and 2 P. M.; the latter being for matinees.

ALCAZAR THEATER, 116 O'Farrell, Vaudeville, 25c, 50c.

Baldwin Theater, 932 Market.
    Every Evening except Sunday; Matinee Saturday.
    Regular Prices, 25, 35, 50, 75c, $1.00 and $1.50.
    Matinee   " $1.00, 75, 50 and 25c.

BAY DISTRICT RACE-TRACK, east side 5th Ave. bet. A and D.

BELLA UNION THEATER, 805 Kearny, variety, 25c and 50c.

BUSH STREET THEATER, 325 Bush, 25, 50, 75c and $1.00.

California Theater, north side Bush bet. Kearny and Dupont.
    Every evening including Sunday; Matinee Saturday.
    Regular Prices, 25, 50, 75c and $1.00.
    Matinee   "   25, 50 and 75c.

CENTRAL PARK, S. E. corner Market and Eighth, athletic grounds.

CHINESE THEATER, 626 Jackson.
        "   (Grand), 814 Washington.
        "   (New), 623 Jackson.
        "   (Royal), 836 Washington.

EDEN MUSEE, 729 Market.

GOLDEN GATE HALL, south side Sutter bet. Taylor and Jones, concert.

GRAND OPERA HOUSE, Mission bet. Third and Fourth, 10, 15, 25 and 50c.

GROVE STREET THEATER, north side Grove bet. Polk and Van Ness Ave., 10, 20 and 30c.

MECHANICS' PAVILION, cor. Larkin and Grove.

METROPOLITAN TEMPLE, east side Fifth bet. Market and Mission, concert.

Midwinter Fair, Golden Gate Park, 50c.

MORROSCO'S THEATER, south side Howard bet. Third and Fourth, 10, 20 and 30c.

NATIONAL THEATER, cor. Eddy and Jones, 10, 20 and 30c.

ORPHEUM, south side O'Farrell bet. Stockton and Powell, Vaudeville, 10, 25 and 50c.

STANDARD THEATER, Bush bet. Montgomery and Kearny, 25, 50 and 75c.

STOCKWELL'S THEATER, Powell, 25, 50, 75c and $1.00.

TIVOLI OPERA HOUSE, Eddy near Market, 25 and 50c.

WIGWAM THEATER, S. E. cor. Stockton and Geary, Vaudeville, 10, 25 and 35c.

PHOTOGRAPHIC CO.

121 Post St. Between Kearny and Grant Avenue — SAN FRANCISCO

OFFICIAL PHOTOGRAPHER

California Midwinter International Exposition, 1894

Studio on Central Court, Exposition Grounds

Bet. the Administration and Mechanical Arts Buildings

The Studio at 121 Post St. is the largest and best equipped Photographic Gallery on the American Continent. The latest improved appliances for producing the finest work by the instantaneous process.

The only Gallery in the world making the CELEBRATED IRIDIUM PHOTOGRAPHS (or Photographs in colors), and at prices nearly as cheap as the ordinary Photograph. The perfection of these pictures is simply marvelous. The visitor is amply repaid by calling and inspecting this beautiful work. Pictures enlarged in crayon, India ink and water colors at moderate prices.

HEADQUARTERS PACIFIC COAST VIEWS

Insurance that Insures

The Provident Savings Life Assurance Society
Of New York

Cash Capital . . $100,000

SHEPPARD HOMANS - - - President and Actuary
WM. E. STEVENS - - - - - - Secretary
CHARLES E. WILLARD - - - Manager of Agencies

The PROVIDENT SAVINGS wrote during the year 1893, in California, a larger business than any other Agency except the "Three Giants."

Allan & Pratt, Managers for Pacific Coast
405 Montgomery St., Cor. California
San Francisco, Cal.

DR. LORYEA'S
Hammam Baths
For Ladies and Gentlemen
212 Post Street

Bet. Grant Avenue and Stockton   *San Francisco*

The Finest Turkish, Russian, Electric and Medicated Baths in this City.

SINGLE BATHS, $1.00   **SIX TICKETS FOR $5.00**

Open for gentlemen, day and night, Sundays included. Open for ladies from 8 A. M. to 6 P. M. Newly renovated throughout. Bath including room, all night, for gentlemen, $1.00.

USE KLINKNER'S PATENT
"Eureka" Self-Inking Stamp Pad
ALL COLORS   NEVER NEEDS INKING
SEND FOR CATALOGUE AND PRICE LIST

C.A. KLINKNER & CO.
→ RED ←
RUBBER STAMPS
STENCILS, BURNING BRANDS,
MEDALS, CHECKS, BOX BRANDS, ETC.
320 Sansome St. San Francisco
TRADE MARK — REGISTERED

The Largest and Most Complete Assortment of Stamps and Stencils on the Coast
USE KLINKNER'S PATENT CABINET FOR
Linen Marking and Card Printing
PRICE, $1.50

CHAS. EIBACH   HENRY KERN
976 CHESTER STREET, OAKLAND   11 LOCUST STREET

Kern & Eibach

INTERIOR DECORATORS

FRESCOING, PAPER HANGING
FREE HAND RELIEF

ROOM 105
Donohoe Building

COR. TAYLOR AND MARKET STS.

SAN FRANCISCO, CAL.

San Francisco

School of Elocution

Voice Building and Dramatic Expression

Your Attention is called to the following Course of Instruction

DISTINCT ARTICULATION
VOICE BUILDING
FACIAL AND PANTOMIMIC EXPRESSION
RECITATION AND READING
ELOCUTION AND ORATORY

LEO COOPER

Saratoga Hall, 814 Geary Street

San Francisco

C. W. R. FORD & CO., 522 Market St, San Francisco

CUTTER'S

SPOOL

SILK

STRONGEST BEST

No Ripped Seams

Wonder! Wonder!

NOVELTIES IN

Millinery

AT THE WONDER

1024, 1026, 1028 Market Street

FEATHERS
FLOWERS
HATS
NEW
VELVETS
LACES
RIBBONS
Etc.

LARGE STOCK   LOW PRICES

Branch

999 Market St., Cor. Sixth St.

SAN FRANCISCO

Branch Stores in OAKLAND and SAN JOSE

LARGEST EXCLUSIVELY MILLINERY
ESTABLISHMENT in the UNITED STATES

"If you don't take the DAILY REPORT you don't get the news."

50 CENTS A MONTH

THE
DAILY REPORT

The People's Paper

Is fearless and independent, and stands first among the evening newspapers of the country. It is by all odds

THE BEST ADVERTISING MEDIUM IN SAN FRANCISCO

And if your "add" is not in it you are making the biggest business mistake of your life.

THE DAILY REPORT HAS

THE LARGEST CIRCULATION

of any paper in San Francisco

Your business languishes because you advertise in dead newspapers that are read by people who are dead and don't know it. The newspaper for you is the

DAILY REPORT

A LIVE NEWSPAPER
READ BY LIVE PEOPLE

Business Office
238 MONTGOMERY STREET

Branch Office
730 MARKET STREET

ARE YOU NEAT? SAVE TEMPER TIME and TROUBLE

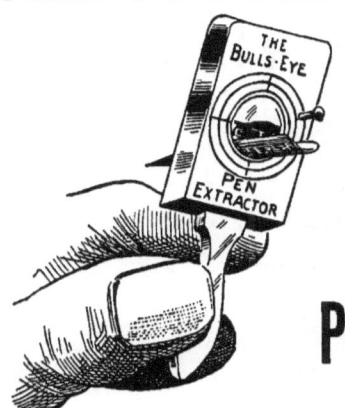

DAYTON'S PATENT BULLS EYE
PEN EXTRACTOR

One Thrust and out comes the Pen

EXTRACTING PEN

It is self-acting, extracting and releasing the pen from the holder instantly

WITHOUT SOILING THE FINGERS

Assorted Styles
Bright Nickel
Dull Silver
Old Bronze

•

Mailed on receipt of price

25 Cts. Each

Special Prices to the Trade
Patented and Patents Pending

PHELPS & DAYTON
15 Drumm St.   San Francisco

RELEASING PEN

At the Fair—Manufacturers and Liberal Arts Building Northeast Corner Gallery

---

J. DOHERTY
Practical Plumber
Gas and Steam Fitter

345 KEARNY STREET

Corner Pine   SAN FRANCISCO, CAL.

Particular Attention Paid to Jobbing of All Kinds
All Work done at the Lowest Rates and Warranted

... TELEPHONE 3040 ...

J. SPAULDING & CO.

Pacific
Cleaning
and Dyeing
Works

Particular Attention Paid to Ladies' and Gents' Clothing . . . . . .

Pioneer Steam Carpet Beating Machines

Sewing and Relaying of Carpets a Specialty. . . . .

353-357 TEHAMA ST., SAN FRANCISCO

A FAIR JUDGE

Is not always reliable—the best way is to buy from a firm who sells honest goods at fair prices—We can fit you to any possible style of Boot or Shoe, as we are direct importers of fine goods, but the anatomical and pedeological qualities of the

DESCALSO $3.00 FOOT FORM SHOE

Is correct. A glance at the Shoe will convince you that we are Headquarters for the best in our line.

DESCALSO BROTHERS

28 KEARNY STREET $3, $4 and $5 Foot Form Shoes

KODAKS

Developed, Printed and Refilled at Reasonable Rates

HEADQUARTERS for VISITORS to the FAIR

Free Dark Rooms, Free Information. Travelers' Orders attended to without delay.

ONE BLOCK

FROM THE

Palace, Grand, Lick, Occidental and California Hotels

R. J. WATERS
COMMERCIAL PHOTOGRAPHER
SAN FRANCISCO

110 SUTTER STREET

THE Evening Bulletin

(Established 1856)

Is the leading evening paper of San Francisco, the recognized authority among bankers, merchants and the entire business community, and reaches the firesides of the best circles, being an irreproachable family journal. It always

CONTAINS

A complete record of all the happenings of 24 hours throughout the entire world and a record you can rely upon. The Bulletin's specialty is not fiction nor sensation. Its specialty is to print

ALL THE NEWS

See the Bulletin and learn how to get $3.00 worth of **"PICTURESQUE CALIFORNIA"** for ten cents.

BUSINESS OFFICE
622 Montgomery Street

Mrs. Ryder

Manicure

126 Kearny St.　　　　　San Francisco
ROOM 48

All Face Preparations for Sale

MICHELS, WAND & CO.

Emporium

FOR

TRIMMINGS & LACES

The Latest European Novelties
in Gloves and Veilings constantly on hand

··o◇o··

MICHELS, WAND & CO.

26 KEARNY ST.　　　　　SAN FRANCISCO

THIS SPACE RESERVED FOR THE

UNION PHOTO-ENGRAVING CO.

581 MISSION STREET, S. F.

Who will soon move into new and larger quarters.
The largest and best equipped house west of Chicago for Half Tone work.

"The Traveler's" Bureau of Information

Located at 602 Market Street, in the State Board of Trade Rooms, keeps on file, for free distribution, printed matter, souvenirs, etc., of all the Hotels and Resorts in the State.

It is their business to furnish WITHOUT CHARGE, reliable information about any Resort, Hotel, Railway or Steamship Line in America, and you are cordially invited to call upon them at any and all times.

YOU WILL FIND THERE

Also, the Office of

"The most beautiful Journal in the United States." It is published monthly, and is profuse in handsome illustrations of California scenery. No Visitor to the Fair should fail to subscribe for it, and it costs only

$1.00 A YEAR

JOHNSTONE & BRYAN, Publishers

602 Market St.   San Francisco, Cal.

W. W. MONTAGUE & CO.

MANUFACTURERS OF

RIVETED STEEL

AND

For Hydraulic Mining, Irrigating, Power Plants, Town and Farm Supply . . . .
Make a Specialty of <u>COATING PIPE</u> with EUREKA Composition . . . .

SEND FOR CATALOGUES

309, 311, 313, 315 AND 317 MARKET STREET, SAN FRANCISCO

www.ingramcontent.com/pod-product-compliance
Lightning Source LLC
Chambersburg PA
CBHW020121170426
43199CB00009B/590